creating
your perfect
quilting space

creating your perfect quilting space

sewing-room makeovers for any space and any budget

LOIS L. HALLOCK

Martingale®
& COMPANY

Creating Your Perfect Quilting Space: Sewing-Room Makeovers for Any Space and Any Budget
© 2005 by Lois L. Hallock

Martingale & Company
20205 144th Avenue NE
Woodinville, WA 98072-8478 USA
www.martingale-pub.com

That Patchwork Place® is an imprint of
Martingale & Company®.

Credits

President	Nancy J. Martin
CEO	Daniel J. Martin
VP and General Manager	Tom Wierzbicki
Publisher	Jane Hamada
Editorial Director	Mary V. Green
Managing Editor	Tina Cook
Technical Editor	Karen Costello Soltys
Copy Editor	Durby Peterson
Design Director	Stan Green
Illustrator	Laurel Strand
Cover and Text Designer	Stan Green
Photographer	Brent Kane

Printed in China
10 09 08 07 06 05   8 7 6 5 4 3 2 1

mission statement

Dedicated to providing quality products
and service to inspire creativity.

dedication

To my parents, who gave me all that I have; for
that I am eternally grateful.

To my husband, Don; your support and love
are what keep me going. Thank you for making
my dreams attainable.

To my children, Jake and Taylor; thank you
for understanding why Mom was so busy while
writing this book. I believe that the passion
that has been awakened in me and expressed
in this book has spilled over and enriched all
our lives. May you grow up to realize your
dreams and passions.

Library of Congress Cataloging-in-Publication Data
Hallock, Lois L.
    Creating your perfect quilting space : sewing-room
makeovers for any space and any budget / Lois L. Hallock.
       p. cm.
    ISBN 1-56477-569-0
    1. Sewing—Equipment and supplies. 2. Quilting—
Equipment and supplies. 3. Workshops—Design and
construction. 4. Artists' studios—Design and construction.
I. Title.
    TT715.H34 2005
    746.46—dc22
                                          2005012744

contents

introduction

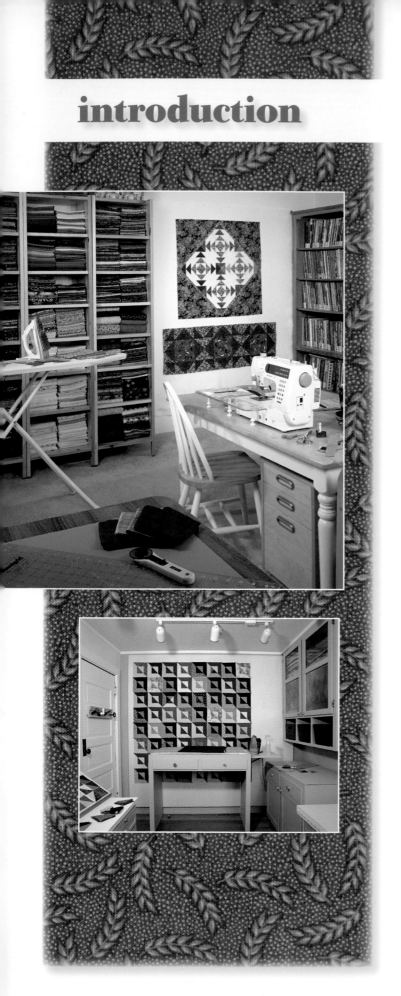

THE FIRST PLACE I WANT TO SEE when I enter a quilter's house is her quilt studio. I can learn so much in just a few glances around the room. Current projects on the wall or cutting table open a discussion of what is happening in our lives. Babies being born, weddings to attend, anniversaries, retirement parties, and memories of someone who has gone—all these are insights into the most important events in our lives. "Who inspired you? What attracted you? Which fabrics leapt off the store shelves into your arms?" The answers tumble into a discussion that could go on for hours.

One of the most surprising things I find when entering some quilt studios is that the quilter has given little attention to important details. It starts with a poor choice in quilt studio location. It continues with furnishings that are less than adequate for working comfortably for long periods. Finally, it culminates in the lack of storage for a fabric stash and quiltmaking tools.

Many quilters tuck themselves away in a corner of a bedroom, in a hallway just barely wide enough for the sewing machine, or in a space they share with a spouse in an already crowded office. Some choose a dark basement near the laundry or a noisy family room. All are trying to fit quilting in around all the other details of life.

The art of quiltmaking deserves to be put closer to the top of your priority list. There are some wonderful ways to combine quilting with the rest of your life so that working on your craft isn't an afterthought. I choose to discard the term *sewing room* and replace it with *quilt studio* or *quilting studio*. Most of us aren't sewing garments for our families to save money. Quiltmaking is an art form; therefore, the creative space deserves the same status as an artist's studio.

Now that I have railed against the terminology we use to define our space, let's move on to what quilters do to themselves by not incorporating ergonomics (or "human-factors engineering") into their studio designs. Women working in the textile industry back in the early eighteen hundreds did not originally have ergonomics designed into their workstations. The long days and repetitive tasks took a toll on their bodies that was permanently disabling. Luckily for us, the science of ergonomics has come along to rescue us from that fate. Simple concepts, such as considering your body height in relation to your sewing machine and cutting surfaces, make a huge difference in how good you feel during quiltmaking. Easy exercises and microbreaks can mean a world of difference in your energy flow.

After you have tackled the basic problems of location and ergonomics, you are left with making your work space efficient and organized. Have you ever noticed that it's so much easier to start a project with a clean work space? How much time do you spend looking for tools or patterns? Have you ever bought the same tool, pattern, or book twice because you just couldn't locate the one you purchased originally? Have you purchased the same fabric twice because you didn't know that you already had it in your stash? All these scenarios are indicators of a problem. But it's not the problem you think—you don't have to stop buying fabric, tools, patterns, or books. Instead, you need to organize what you have.

In this book I will show you how to reorganize your quilt studio to maximize your creative energy. You will learn the importance of ergonomics and room layout, along with good storage techniques. Ultimately you will save time and money while reducing stress, bringing out the quilt artist that lives within you.

the basics of quilt studio design

IT HELPS TO UNDERSTAND SOME BASIC CONCEPTS before designing your perfect quilt studio. My work in a factory environment has taught me some basics of human factors that easily apply to the quilt studio. Well-planned work environments that have a lot of natural lighting with well-organized tools and supplies stimulate productivity. In this chapter you will learn how to select your best possible work location, use the work-triangle concept, make it easy to locate tools and supplies, choose appropriate lighting, and improve your quilting ergonomics.

location, location, location

As in home buying, location is the most important thing to consider in the design of your quilt studio. Hiding your studio in the farthest corner of your house, attic, or basement implies that quilting is a low priority. Putting your studio in the corner of a multiuse room is also not necessarily ideal. Consider your individual needs and daily schedule.

Natural light is one of the first considerations when selecting a room that will suit your needs—assuming you have the ability to choose any room in the house with no other constraints. Painters, sculptors, and other artists tend to design studios with a lot of windows or skylights. You can and should use full-spectrum artificial light if you can't design enough natural light into your studio.

Square footage is also an important consideration. A quilt studio that is cramped and physically constrained will make producing large quilts

This quilt studio is flooded with natural daylight in the afternoons, but supplemental full-spectrum lighting is needed for early morning and evening sewing.

difficult. A larger quilt studio provides more work space and storage capabilities.

consider your needs

The ideal location of your quilting studio is determined by how you wish to fit quilting into your daily life. Some of this choice is based on needs and some of it is based on personality. The needs-based side of the issue deals with where you need to spend your time. If you have young children at home when you are quilting, you may wish to have your quilting studio in the family room or playroom. If your children are grown, you may wish to have a more private space. Similarly, if you are caring for an elderly family member, you may wish to be where you can hear when you are needed. Also, if you intend to fit quiltmaking around cooking dinner or doing laundry, maybe closer proximity to the kitchen or laundry room would make sense. Certainly, fabric prewashing would be more convenient if the laundry room were nearby.

consider your personality

The personality based side of the location issue has to do with you. Do you like to be the center of action or do you prefer to work alone? Some people thrive on activity and interaction; they have a TV or music playing in the background during every activity. They prefer a changing environment and draw energy from other people. Others need serenity and solitude to create, recharging in a room alone with their favorite things.

the work triangle

The work triangle is a concept that has been used successfully in kitchen design for many years. The basic premise is that when working in the kitchen, you move most frequently between three major workstations: the range, the refrigerator, and the sink. A logical arrangement of these workstations will improve your efficiency as you prepare meals.

Most books suggest keeping the work triangle as small as possible in order to shorten the distance that you travel when moving between stations. But there are some limits to how small one should make a work triangle. You need work surfaces between these stations in order to prepare food or stage ingredients. It follows that a bigger kitchen is not always better; if it's poorly laid out, it can be worse. Well-designed gourmet kitchens incorporate *more* work triangles, not *larger* ones.

Quilters typically move between their sewing machine, cutting mat, and ironing board. These three workstations constitute the quilter's work triangle. Consider carefully where you are performing these separate tasks. Are they occurring in close proximity to each other? Or is your cutting table in a separate room from your sewing machine?

Some quilters are not fortunate enough to have a dedicated space for quilting. If that's your case, you'll need to have portable workstations that you can set up temporarily and take down easily for stowing. The principles of arranging your workstations in a triangle apply to a temporary setup as well as a permanent studio.

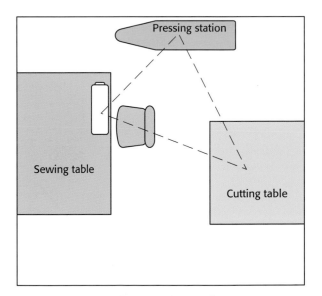

Quilter's work triangle

kitting tools and supplies

Along with minimizing the distance you need to travel between the points of your work triangle, another way to improve your efficiency is to pack or store tools and supplies together in see-through containers or open baskets. Wasting time and energy searching for items each time you perform a task will quickly reduce any efficiency you've gained by arranging your studio in a work triangle. In kitchen design, you put your cooking utensils, pots, and pans near the stove; your dish soap and sponges near the sink; and your storage containers near the refrigerator. The closer an item is to the place where it is needed, the better.

In industry, we call this *kitting*, having all the tools and supplies where you need them. Here are some suggestions for kitting tools and supplies in your quilting studio.

at the sewing machine

Keep all thread, machine feet, pins, and scissors nearby. If your sewing table doesn't have drawers for this purpose, a simple rolling office cart would suffice. If the sewing table is near a wall, consider a peg-board, thread rack, or other wall organizer. If you need something more portable, try a tackle box, toolbox, or desktop organizer.

at the cutting table

Rotary cutters and rulers need to be accessible. Look for ruler racks and baskets in quilt shops and sewing-notions catalogs. Another option is to hang rulers from a peg-board if wall space is available. My favorite solution is a cutting table with low-profile drawers (similar to the printer's trays or architectural drawing tables used in industry). The drawers allow you to sort your rulers and templates along with marking pens and graph paper for quilt design.

Wooden cutlery trays are great for kitting cutting tools. The dividers keep tools separated and visible, while the handle makes it easy to grab a tray and go.

at the pressing station

Locate spray starch, water for the iron, pressing sheets, and pins where you can easily reach them. Notions suppliers and home-organization catalogs offer wall racks, shelves, and ironing board covers with pockets for storage. All can be good solutions, depending on your work style and needs.

visual controls

What does this mean? Simply put, visual controls are labels, pictures, or outlines of your tools showing their location. They're very helpful in making sure you have everything you need when you start a task. How many times have you gone to the drawer, toolbox, or pocket where you store your rotary cutter or scissors and found that the item you wanted grew legs?

cues for tool storage

One simple way to incorporate visual controls in your studio is to use a brightly colored or white pen to outline every tool on a peg-board. When you glance at your peg-board, you can see instantly if something is missing. This allows you to retrieve the item before you get engrossed in a task. Of course, some discipline is required here. You'll need to care enough to put supplies and tools back where they belong when you're finished with them for the day.

cues for book and magazine storage

When storing magazines and books, labeling shelves or storage boxes with the contents will improve your ability to retrieve materials needed for design tasks. Grouping books by similar topics can help when you want to consult them for ideas.

cues for project storage

Visual controls are also a benefit when it comes to storing works in progress (WIP). I have heard quilters refer to works in progress as UFOs or unfinished objects. I prefer the term *works in progress* rather than *unfinished objects*. An unfinished object is something that is in need of finishing.

Works in progress have no time limit, and this expression has no negative connotation.

Many quilters have experienced the benefit of having WIP available when a sudden need for a gift arises, such a being invited to a baby shower. Storing WIP in labeled boxes will help you locate a project. Photos and fabric samples pasted on the outside of boxes are great cues to what is stored inside each box.

cues for fabric storage

My favorite visual control is used in fabric storage. Said simply, I like to see all my fabric at once. I sort mostly by colors of the rainbow and somewhat by style. When I need a certain color for a project, I can quickly locate the place where it would be. This works really well during the design phase of a project when I am selecting the color palette. A well-sorted stash increases the likelihood that you will use what you have on hand rather than purchase new fabric for every project. One quilter I know said she uses a color-sorting technique to help her decide what color families she needs to replenish on shopping trips.

This collection of novelty fabrics is organized by themes such as fruits and vegetables, holidays, and juvenile prints to help the quilter keep track of what she has.

lighting

If there is one thing I have come to appreciate more as I age, it is having the correct amount of light for performing a task. You may not even realize that your lighting levels are too low; you may simply find yourself annoyed with certain tasks that involve smaller pieces or that require more accuracy. A person at age 40 may require twice as much light as a person at age 20.

Ambient lighting is the general lighting that you use to illuminate a room, and is often a ceiling light operated from a light switch as you enter the room. *Task lighting* is the directed light that you use for a specific task such as reading, cutting fabric, or sewing. Typically, task lighting is brighter and more focused than ambient lighting.

Light bulbs usually have three performance values quoted on their packaging: light output in lumens, energy usage in watts, and life in hours. Lower wattages and longer life help reduce power costs, but watts and hours do not directly tell you the amount of light the bulb will generate. Lumens are more important for determining the amount of light a given bulb will provide.

Be aware that the amount of light measured at your work surface depends on two factors: how bright your bulb is (how many lumens it puts out) and how far your bulb is from your work surface. In other words, replacing overhead light bulbs with high-lumen bulbs will improve your ambient light levels, but may not significantly improve the task lighting at your cutting table.

Building codes for residential housing require only that installed lighting provide sufficient ambient light to move around in a room without running into things or tripping. Newly constructed houses typically provide the minimum ambient light levels in bedrooms, family rooms, and living rooms. Typical office buildings are designed with four times that level. Office and manufacturing space designed to accommodate tasks that are very detailed and that include color matching require 10 times the basic residential ambient lighting levels. So quilting can require up to 10 times more light for task lighting than what probably exists in your room as ambient lighting.

In addition to the appropriate amount of light, quilters also need to consider the quality of their light source. Ultimately, natural light is best because it represents the full spectrum of colors. The term *full-spectrum lighting* has come to represent a light source that most closely mimics natural daylight, allowing accurate color rendering. Many quilters and other artists locate their studios in the room with the most windows and skylights so they can take advantage of the full-spectrum light freely available during daylight hours. Of course, unless you want to quilt only in daylight hours, even the sunniest quilt studio will need supplemental lighting.

choosing the right bulbs

Before you rush out to replace all the light bulbs in your studio, there are two important factors to consider in choosing the right type of bulbs. The two terms *Color Temperature* and *Color Rendering Index (CRI)* are used by the lighting industry to describe the quality of light in relation to daylight. Color Temperature describes the appearance, atmosphere, and ambiance or mood created by the light and is measured in degrees Kelvin. Standard incandescent light sources measure at 2700 K. In comparison, daylight measures at 6500 K. Therefore, a higher color temperature is needed to mimic natural light. When shopping for replacement bulbs for your quilt studio, buy the highest Color Temperature bulbs you can find to achieve the closest match to natural light.

Color Rendering Index is the ability of a light source to produce natural colors in objects. CRI is measured on a scale from 0 to 100 where 100 is the best. The higher the CRI, the more natural the people and objects will appear. Most standard incandescent bulbs have a CRI of 60, and standard fluorescent bulbs have a CRI of 60–75. Quilting studios should use light sources of 80 CRI and above. The table on the facing page compares light bulbs that have a CRI of over 80 that are found in the average hardware store.

In addition to the brands listed in the table, many bulb manufacturers marketing full-spectrum lighting to quilters and crafters offer compact fluorescent bulbs with a CRI of around 95. Be aware that bulbs advertised as "full-spectrum" profess to mimic daylight, but they're not guaranteed to have good color rendering, so check the label before buying.

task lighting

Each point of the quilter's work triangle requires its own dedicated task lighting, with the cutting table needing the most light. Be aware that if you locate the light source behind your head, you will have the shadow of your head falling right on your work surface. Articulating lamps allow you to position your light source without shadows.

Clamp-on desk lamps with adjustable, articulating arms allow you to move the light around depending on the current task. Your lamp should be able to reach any point on your table. A floor lamp with articulation also works for most tasks. Built-in surfaces, however, may benefit most from under-cabinet lighting or hanging fixtures.

Most sewing machines have their own built-in lights to illuminate the needle area of the machine. I find this to be sufficient task lighting at my sewing machine during daylight hours. At night I use a portable full-spectrum lamp to provide more task lighting for my sewing table. My pressing station

has the least amount of task lighting in my quilting studio. I generally use my iron for pressing seams, which requires relatively little lighting. Quilters who use their iron to do fusible appliqué would want more light. Bringing your portable floor lamp to your ironing station when doing tasks that require higher light levels is a simple solution.

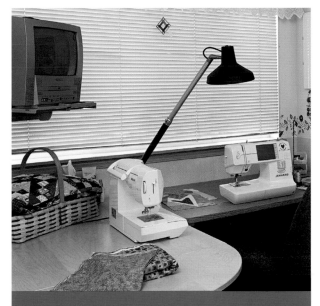

An articulated task lamp makes it easy to direct additional light on either the sewing machine or the embroidery machine in this studio.

light bulb comparisons

Type of Light Bulb	Manufacturer	Model	Light Output (Lumens)	Color Temperature (Kelvin)	Color Rendering Index (CRI)
Incandescent	GE	Soft White 60W A lamp	660	2764 K	100
	Sylvania	INC 3277K	Unspecified	3279 K	100
Compact Fluorescent	GE	FLE15TBX/L/LLCD	900	2653 K	83
	Greenlite	ELS-M 15W	900	2702 K	82
	Sylvania	CF20EL/Twist	1200	2977 K	82
	Westinghouse	SKU 37351	900	2938 K	81
T8 Fluorescent (24" long)	GE	F32T8/SP35 Trimline	2848	3354 K	81
	GE	F32T8SPX50	2816	4751 K	87
	Phillips	F32T8/TL735 Hi-Vision	2944	3370 K	84
	Verilux	F32T8VLX	2816	6369 K	85

Source: Rea, Mark, Lei Deng, and Robert Wolsey, "Full-Spectrum Light Sources," *Lighting Answers* 7, no. 5 (2003).

If you have a large quilt studio with multiple workstations, you may want to consider installing track lighting or a hanging fixture over each workstation. Each of the major bulb manufacturers has high CRI fluorescent, compact tube, or halogen lights available. To avoid having to run new wiring for your new lighting, make sure to choose fixtures that will run off of your standard supply voltage. If you have a small studio, replacing your task-lamp bulbs with compact fluorescents may solve your lighting issues. Be aware that most full-spectrum and compact-tube lights do not work on dimmer switches.

the downside of light

Natural light and full-spectrum light bulbs share more than just the ability to render color accurately. They both will fade fabric that is exposed to them. Some new full-spectrum light sources provide ultraviolet (UV) protection. Since this is a relatively new development in natural lighting options, most quilters have bulbs that produce UV rays. Therefore, they should store fabric behind closed doors or away from direct light sources so that it doesn't fade.

ergonomics

Ergonomics is a relatively new field of science that combines knowledge from engineering and medicine to make equipment and furnishings more human-friendly.

An ergonomic assessment of your quilting studio can help you determine how to maximize comfort during your time in your studio. While the scope of ergonomics is quite vast, I use a few simple rules of thumb when making a preliminary assessment of a quilter's studio.

neutral position

One of the key concepts of ergonomics is keeping your body in a neutral position as much as possible. Neutral position is the most relaxed state for your body. Your weight is centered and your limbs are relaxed. Whether sitting or standing, your body should be centered on your work. Many sewing tables are designed to fold into the smallest space

possible, and often the design does not allow the quilter to sit with her body at the centerline of the needle. This sideways displacement of the quilter's spine for long periods results in discomfort and fatigue. If your table does not have sufficient legroom on either side of the needle centerline, consider replacing it with a table that does.

sewing machine height and adjustment

Much research has been focused on the ergonomic height for keyboarding at a computer. Luckily for quilters, comfortable keyboard height is very similar to comfortable machine-sewing height. If you have an average torso length, your machine bed should be about 9" above the seat of your chair. This measurement does vary from person to person, so follow the guidelines in the diagram below for sitting with good posture. Ask a friend or family member to look at your profile while you are seated and evaluate you to see if your machine height is correct for your body.

Many quilters have discovered that tilting their machines toward them improves their comfort and ability to see their work, especially during machine quilting. This is similar to the tilt of most drafting tables. One disadvantage to a sloped sewing table is that tools are more likely to slide off. I have seen quilters use purchased tilting platforms or wedge-shaped door stops under their machines to achieve better viewing angles while maintaining a flat table surface for their tools. Be careful not to tilt your machine or table so far that it may tip over during use.

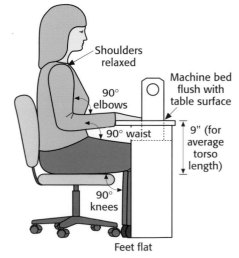

Ergonomics of machine sewing

chair adjustment

Since very few sewing tables are adjustable for height, be sure to choose a chair with adjustable seat height and backrest position. Your seat needs to be adjusted so that when your arms and shoulders are relaxed, your palms can rest on the sewing machine bed with your elbows forming a 90° angle.

The backrest should be adjusted so that your lower back has good lumbar support. When you are seated at the sewing machine, your hips and knees should also rest comfortably at 90° angles. If the heels of your feet do not touch the floor when the rest of your body is positioned correctly at your sewing table, you need a footrest to raise your foot pedal.

cutting table height

Cutting table height is critical to comfort when you are rotary cutting for long periods of time. For most average-sized adults, ideal cutting height while standing is similar to the height of kitchen countertops. This is not a coincidence. It turns out that the ideal height for using a knife to chop vegetables is the same as the ideal height for using a rotary cutter to cut fabric. The average kitchen cabinet supports countertops at a finished height of 36". Unfortunately, most quilters start by using a dining table, an extra folding table, or an office desk for rotary cutting. All of these surfaces are usually about 30" high. Only a quilter who is very small in stature can stand and comfortably cut on a 30"-high table. The rest of us start to get a backache after a very short time cutting.

The distance from your elbow to the ground when you are standing with shoulders relaxed is key to selecting a cutting table that is sized to you. Have a friend or family member do the measuring for you, because we tend to measure a bit low when doing it alone. Your cutting surface should be about 6" lower than your elbow height. This will feel high at first, but as you adjust to the new height you will find yourself becoming less fatigued while cutting.

Most quilters like to have a cutting table where they can stand as they make their initial fabric

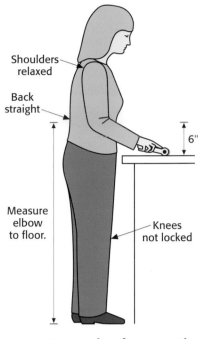

Ergonomics of rotary cutting

Shoulders relaxed

Back straight

6"

Measure elbow to floor.

Knees not locked

cuts. This is because a long reach is necessary to rotary cut across a 20"-wide folded piece of fabric. Your reach when standing at the correct-height table is about 35", while your reach when seated drops to about 16". As you reach farther from your body, your arm becomes less stable and you lose both accuracy and the ability to provide the correct downward pressure to rotary cut effectively.

After making initial cuts while standing, some quilters cut small pieces while seated at their sewing machine (a secondary cutting station). A task chair that swivels and rolls on a hard surface can be very efficient for moving between sewing and secondary cutting stations. In this case, the ergonomic solution is to set the chair height for comfortable sewing and use a surface that is a few inches lower for comfortable cutting.

ironing board height

Most ironing boards are adjustable to allow you to set the right height for your body. A comfortable ironing height is about 3" taller than a comfortable cutting height, because an iron is heavier than a rotary cutter. In order to avoid injury and fatigue, heavy items should be handled as close to your body's center as possible. If your ironing board is set too low, you'll tend to bend over and involve your back in the lifting motions. If your ironing board is too high, you will be lifting with your shoulders. An ironing board or pressing surface needs to be just a few inches below your elbows while you are standing.

Ergonomics of pressing

In addition to a secondary cutting station, many quilters use a secondary pressing station while seated at their sewing machine. They use their primary pressing station to press fabric yardage after prewashing it and to press quilts while piecing rows, but use their secondary station for pressing individual pieces and blocks before assembling the quilt. This allows the quilter to have multiple work triangles that are useful for different tasks. Some use a smaller iron and ironing pad on a nearby table, again rolling between workstations on an office chair. Pressing while seated is similar to cutting while seated, and a surface a few inches lower than your machine bed is recommended. Remember that your reach while seated is limited to 16", so secondary cutting or pressing stations are better placed so they are perpendicular to your sewing table (in an L formation) rather than side by side as shown in illustration above right.

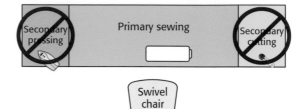

Do place secondary cutting and pressing areas in a U-shaped layout.

Don't place secondary cutting and pressing areas in a straight line.

storage height

Height also needs to be considered when you're seeking storage solutions. Heavy items should be stored no lower than your knees and no higher than your shoulders. Reserve the higher and lower shelves for lightweight and less-used items. Also, you will notice that your ability to reach an item on a deep shelf varies depending on the height of the shelf. A shoulder-high shelf can be as deep as your arm is long, and you can still reach the back of the shelf. You can reach only the front of shelves that are above shoulder height.

Because most quilting supplies are not excessively heavy, storage height is usually based on what we can easily see. A good rule of thumb is to store the items you use the most at eye level so that you can find what you need more quickly and with less searching.

Ergonomics is not just about surface heights, but making sure that your work surfaces are the proper height is a good place to start when setting up your space. After you have the surface heights solved in your work triangle, you need to think next about tool placement. Twisting, stretching, or taking unnecessary steps while performing any task will wear you out over time. Rotary

cutters and rulers should be in easy reach from your cutting stations. Similarly, pressing supplies should be in easy reach from your ironing station, and sewing supplies should be right where you need them at your sewing station. If you use both standing and seated stations, you may wish to have two sets of some supplies, larger ones at the primary station and smaller equivalents at the secondary station. Any wasted motion lowers your efficiency during any task.

stretching and microbreaks

Quilters move steadily in their work triangle without staying very long in one position or at one station. This is the most comfortable and ergonomic way to work. Occasionally quilters work on a project that requires several hours of initial cutting. The maximum time spent standing at any task should be 30 minutes. After that, you should either take a break or switch to a different task that allows you to sit for a while. Standing for long periods is hard on your back and legs.

Similarly, machine quilting at a standard sewing machine may require a quilter to sit in one position for a long period of time. Frequent breaks with neck and shoulder stretching will increase your longevity at that task. Concentrate on keeping your muscles relaxed, with your arms in as neutral a position as possible while quilting. Tense muscles will reduce your accuracy and shorten your effective quilting time. Some quilters experience muscle aches the day after performing a particularly long session of machine quilting. Stretching and taking 5-minute microbreaks every 30 minutes will reduce the likelihood of muscle aches.

Ergonomics is all about being comfortable while working or playing. It is about preventing injury and working without pain. It is about enjoying yourself and being efficient. Efficient and comfortable quilting leads you to be productive and creative. An understanding of the basic concepts of work triangles, visual controls, and ergonomics sets the stage for assessing your situation.

assessing your situation

BY NOW YOU ARE PROBABLY WONDERING just how to go about putting all of this knowledge together to create your perfect quilting studio. By following some simple steps and doing some up-front legwork, you'll be able to sit down and design your studio. The first step is to do a self assessment that will help you identify your biggest problems and focus on solving them.

I use a questionnaire when I first meet with a quilter so I can get to know her needs and understand her style. The basic questions you will ask yourself during the assessment are:

- What are my biggest problems with my existing studio?
- What do I like most about my existing studio?
- What are my location constraints or preferences?
- Are my surfaces the right heights?
- What am I keeping?
- What can I get rid of?
- Do I want to see my fabric all the time?
- Does my furniture need to be built in, free standing, or portable?
- Does my furniture need to match existing furniture, flooring, or molding?
- Is my lighting sufficient?
- What is my budget?

As you were reading the previous chapter, you may have been getting some ideas on how to improve your quilt studio. Take the time to answer the above questions on paper so you will have some focus as you proceed. Prioritize your needs so you can concentrate on the most important items first, while staying within your budget.

Most quilters approach me with the belief that their biggest problem is lack of storage. However, they're unaware that they may be injuring their bodies due to the lack of ergonomic considerations. So, I often suggest to my clients to make the ergonomics of surface heights their first priority. Your comfort level will improve your enjoyment—and hopefully your longevity.

ergonomics assessment

Spend some time in your quilt studio investigating the ergonomics of your room. Have a friend analyze your profile and take measurements following the guidelines in the previous chapter and write them in the box below. If ideal heights are more than one inch different from your actual heights, consider modifying or replacing your work surfaces.

Sewing Machine Bed Height

Actual: _____ Ideal: _____

Cutting Surface Height

Actual: _____ Ideal: _____

Pressing Surface Height:

Actual: _____ Ideal: _____

location and layout

Consider whether you are in the best possible room in your house for quilting. Is there another room with better lighting or more square footage that is located closer to the space where you spend most of your time? Can you combine your quilting space with a low-use room like a guest room or formal living room? Is there a large room in the house that you can divide into multiple uses?

Making a layout drawing of your quilt studio will help you audition new furniture and easily play with changing the location of your existing furniture.

Step 1: Using ¼" graph paper, draw a scale model of the room you have chosen for your quilting studio. Measure every wall, window, and door in inches. I find it easiest to use ¼" graph paper and draw to the scale of 2 squares = 1 foot. Using a ruler and mechanical pencil gives me the best results. Mark the locations of the electrical outlets, light switches, heating registers, and light fixtures on this plan view of your studio. Don't

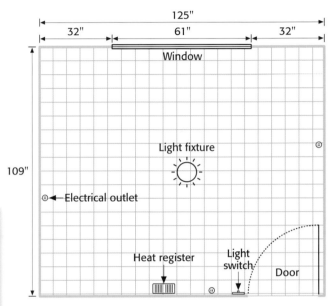

Plan view of quilt studio

Ceiling height = 96"
Window height from floor = 41"
Window height = 42"
Space above window to ceiling = 13"

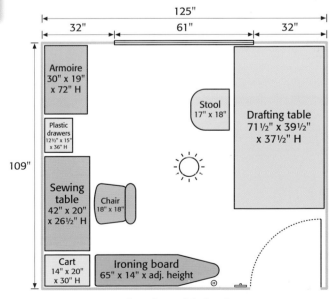

Plan view with furniture

forget to put the dimensions on the drawing so you can refer to them later. It helps to record the ceiling height and window height for fitting furniture into your studio.

Step 2: Measure each piece of furniture that is in your studio. Draw a scale model of each furniture piece on graph paper. Be sure you use the same scale in making these models. Glue the graph paper patterns to card stock and cut out the scale models of your furniture pieces. I find it helpful to use colored index cards and a glue stick for this step, and I like to use the same color for all furniture pieces that are used for the same task.

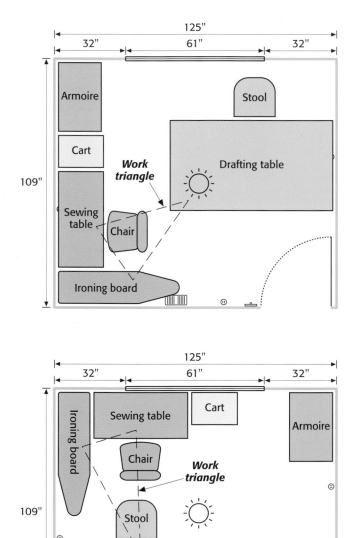

Label each of these models as to what it is and what its dimensions are.

Step 3: Put your furniture models in the same location on your plan view as they are in your studio.

Step 4: Now move the furniture models around to audition new layouts without having to actually move furniture. Spend a few minutes playing with these pieces. Pay particular attention to the size of your work triangle as you assess these different designs. It's possible that your new studio is just a rearrangement of what you already own. Pay attention to heat register, window, and door locations when moving pieces. These tend to be items you won't want to relocate due to the high costs of moving a door or rerouting heating ducts.

storage needs

To get an accurate assessment of just how much storage space you'll need, take an inventory of your fabric, books, patterns, batting, and anything else that you want to store in your quilting studio. Use the specific measuring directions below and record all the dimensions on the Quilter's Needs Assessment Worksheet, opposite.

Fabric. Measure all the fabric you have. I am not kidding. Most quilters that I work with are stunned by this. But you need to know how much storage will be required to keep all your fabric in one place. Look under the bed, in the spare bedroom closet, in the garage, and in all the other places you may have been stashing fabric because your storage system has overflowed.

So you ask, "How do I measure all my fabric?" Start by measuring the volume that your fabric fills. (Volume = length x width x height.) If you have it stored in multiple places, add up the various volumes to get the final answer. If you have boxes of fabric, you can measure the length, width, and height of each box. Multiply the dimensions to get the volume of the box. Then add together the volume of each box to come up with a total volume. If you have fabric on shelving, you can measure the length and depth of the shelving and estimate the height of the stacks.

Quilter's Needs Assessment Worksheet

Fabric Volume

Box/Shelf #1	Length _____	x Width _____	x Height _____	= _____
Box/Shelf #2	Length _____	x Width _____	x Height _____	= _____
Box/Shelf #3	Length _____	x Width _____	x Height _____	= _____
Box/Shelf #4	Length _____	x Width _____	x Height _____	= _____
Box/Shelf #5	Length _____	x Width _____	x Height _____	= _____
Box/Shelf #6	Length _____	x Width _____	x Height _____	= _____
Box/Shelf #7	Length _____	x Width _____	x Height _____	= _____

Total = _____

Book and Magazine Space

Stack/Shelf #1	Length _____
Stack/Shelf #2	Length _____
Stack/Shelf #3	Length _____
Stack/Shelf #4	Length _____
Stack/Shelf #5	Length _____
Stack/Shelf #6	Length _____
Stack/Shelf #7	Length _____
	Total = _____

Pattern Space

Stack/Shelf #1	Length _____
Stack/Shelf #2	Length _____
Stack/Shelf #3	Length _____
Stack/Shelf #4	Length _____
Stack/Shelf #5	Length _____
	Total = _____

UFOs or WIP Quantity

Unfinished quilt tops (number)	_____
Block collections (number)	_____
Fabric collections waiting to be quilts (number)	_____
Total UFOs/WIP	_____

Scrap Volume

Box #1	Length _____	x Width _____	x Height _____	= _____
Box #2	Length _____	x Width _____	x Height _____	= _____
Box #3	Length _____	x Width _____	x Height _____	= _____

Total = _____

Batting Volume

Box #1	Length _____	x Width _____	x Height _____	= _____
Box #2	Length _____	x Width _____	x Height _____	= _____
Box #3	Length _____	x Width _____	x Height _____	= _____

Total = _____

Special Storage Needs

Number of fabric bolts	_____
Number of batting rolls	_____
Large items	_____

Ideal Furniture Heights

Ideal sewing machine bed height	_____
Ideal cutting surface height	_____
Ideal pressing surface height	_____

Determine your fabric volume by measuring and then multiplying the length by depth by height of your shelves. Don't forget to measure the amount of fabric you have stashed elsewhere too.

UFOs or WIP. Count your started projects and record them on your worksheet. Unfinished quilt tops take up more space, so they need to be counted separately from block collections and fabric collections waiting to become quilts.

Scraps. Measure the volume of scraps that you have saved. Again, multiply length by width by height to get volume. Boxes are easier to measure than bags, so put your bag in a box to measure volume and record it on your worksheet.

Batting. Measure the volume of batting that you keep on hand. Again, it is easier to measure boxes than to measure bags of batting. Stuff your batting in a box to measure it. Add up the box volumes to get a total batting volume and record it.

Special storage needs. Some items are just so large or bulky that they require special consideration for storage. Large rolls of batting or whole bolts of fabric will require extra space in your studio. Multiple sewing machines, multiple machine covers, or luggage for traveling with mats or machines take up extra space. Count these items now and record them on your worksheet so you remember to plan for them in your new studio design.

If measuring and recording your quilt studio contents has been an extremely painful experience, you should seriously consider reducing your storage needs by donating unused items to your guild or local thrift store. As in any organizing task, the hardest step is sorting items into one of three categories: use it all the time, may use it sometimes, or will most likely never use it. Rid yourself of the items you will never use. Someone else will be very happy to get items that are just taking up space in your studio. The most thrilling part of this experience is clearing space to bring in fresh new fabrics or books.

In the example shown in the plan view on page 19, this quilter stored all her fabric in her armoire. The armoire measured 30" x 19" x 72" for a total of 41,040 cubic inches of space for fabric. As you can see in the photo of this actual armoire, it is completely full. However, only about half of the contents are quilting fabrics. Stashed behind the other door are wool fabrics, quilt batting, and more. If your cabinet is not full of fabric, you can estimate fabric volume by multiplying by the percentage that *is* full (e.g., if half full, multiply by 0.5). Calculate your fabric volume and write it on the needs assessment worksheet on page 21.

Books and magazines. Stack your books and measure how high the stack is. If the stack is too high, add together the heights of multiple stacks. If they are already on shelving, just measure the length of shelf each stack takes up and add up the lengths. Record this on your worksheet.

Patterns. Measure how much shelf space your patterns take up when they're standing vertically. Record the measurements and total them on your worksheet.

finding the right solutions

YOUR NEWLY DESIGNED QUILTING STUDIO needs to be centered on the important tasks that you do while quilting, which are the three points of the work triangle: sewing, cutting, and pressing. We will look at improving each of these task areas along with improving storage.

sewing table options

Most sewing tables on the market are not adjustable in height. Unless you are exactly the size person that these tables are made for, it is likely that they are the wrong height for your body. Most of the ones I have found are too high, causing quilters to tense their shoulders while sewing. If you already have a sewing table and you don't want to replace it, your best bet is to adjust your chair higher to meet the correct body positioning as described on page 14 and use a platform for your feet and foot pedal.

Platform

Another common table choice by quilters is a banquet table or office desk for sewing. Most of these are not adjustable in height either. Since the sewing machine sits on top (rather than with the machine bed flush with the table surface), the machine bed is likely to be too high relative to your body position. Again, short of replacing the sewing table entirely, your best option is to raise your chair and use a foot platform.

If you are not satisfied with your sewing table, or if a foot platform doesn't work for you, you could buy an adjustable-height table or buy table legs the height you want and make your own tabletop for a custom fit. Used with a Sew Steady machine-bed extender, an adjustable table is an inexpensive solution.

Another option is to have a custom-height sewing table built for you. Most custom cabinet and furniture makers will adjust their standard designs to your dimensions and specifications.

My favorite design choice for a sewing station is a U-shaped work space. Some of the commercially available sewing tables incorporate pullout shelves or flip-down extensions to create a U-shaped surface. The advantage to this design is that it maximizes the surface area that is easy to reach from your seated position. If you are using desks or banquet tables, you may be able to accomplish the same benefits by positioning multiple tables, small rollout carts, clamp-on pressing tables, or ironing boards set to a low height.

The U-shaped workstation lets you keep a small cutting mat and ironing pad to the right and left of your sewing machine. With a swivel task chair on wheels, you can move quickly and easily through a miniature work triangle. This is the ultimate in efficiency—no more jumping up to press one seam or trim one block. Nearly every makeover featured in this book incorporates a U-shaped workstation, regardless of the room size.

If you are considering replacing your sewing table or adding rolling carts for cutting and pressing, make new index-card paper models of your ideal U-shaped sewing station to use on your graph paper room layout.

cutting table options

Having a small cutting mat at your sewing station gives you easy access for small cutting tasks, but it does not eliminate the need for a good cutting table. I prefer a minimum surface size of 36" x 24" for cutting. This allows me to lay out an entire yard of fabric (folded selvage to selvage) at once.

Most commercially available cutting tables are made to fold smaller when not in use and therefore do not include good use of storage space underneath. A lot of quilters leave their collapsible cutting tables open permanently and do not need them to fold smaller. If this is the case, the space underneath is just wasted. If you plan to leave your cutting table up permanently, you may want to consider another piece of furniture that combines a cutting surface with good underneath storage.

As discussed earlier, cutting table height is dependent on your elbow height when measured from the floor. While most tables are too short for the average quilter to use for cutting, a lot of quilters can comfortably cut at the height of a kitchen counter. Kitchen cabinets include some nice features that work well for quilters. They are usually 24" deep, tend have drawers for tools and supplies, provide underneath storage, and incorporate a recessed kickplate that allows you to stand with your toes slightly underneath the cabinet, thereby relieving stress on your lower back.

Kitchen cabinets can be expensive, but other freestanding kitchen furnishings offer many of the same features and are less expensive. Rolling microwave carts or kitchen islands with fold-up table extensions are very good for cutting. They generally come in standard kitchen heights and often have locking castors to make them portable. I don't recommend ones with marble or metal surfaces, because cutting mats may slip easily.

Sideboards or buffets are also usually a good height and incorporate handy drawers for tools and supplies. However, you may need to add your own larger tabletop to get the 24" depth you need for a cutting mat.

A bedroom dresser is another alternative for a cutting surface. Dressers come in a multitude of sizes and have lots of storage drawers. Garage sales can be a great place to find inexpensive furniture

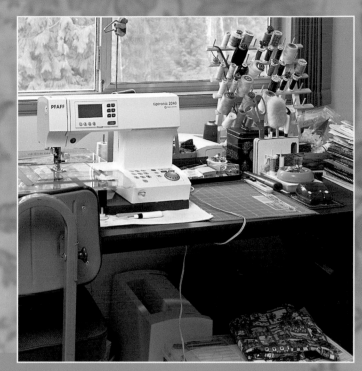

A clamp-on table or rolling cart is an easy way to increase your work space when sewing at an office or banquet table.

Reaching around your machine to access a pressing pad or cutting mat adds strain to your sewing session.

A pine extension was added to the back of this buffet, making it the right size for a cutting mat and providing concealed storage space below.

Some buffet tables and base kitchen cabinets are the perfect height for rotary cutting. This one features storage drawers as well as open shelving.

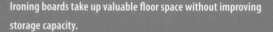
Ironing boards take up valuable floor space without improving storage capacity.

A purchased buffet offers something ironing boards don't—lots of bulk storage! Simply add a homemade top covered in heat- and moisture-resistant fabric.

that meets your needs. Remember to go armed with your tape measure, ideal surface height, and favorite cutting mat dimensions so you get the correct height, depth, and width.

An inexpensive and portable solution to the cutting table height problem can be adjustable-height table-leg extenders. You can make your own out of PVC pipe or purchase ready-made ones that are adjustable (see "Product Sources" on page 94). My guild uses these extensions on quilt retreats to create ergonomic-height cutting tables out of regular banquet tables. After adding these extenders, be certain that your cutting surface is stable before using it.

If you are considering replacing your cutting table, make an index-card model of your ideal cutting table for use in your graph paper layout. Make it as big as your largest cutting mat with some extra room for a ruler rack or tool basket.

pressing station options

Having a small pressing station that you can reach while seated at your sewing table is certainly handy, but it does not replace the need for a larger

pressing surface. The vast majority of quilters use a standard ironing board for pressing. Most ironing boards are height adjustable, but that is where their advantages end. They take up a lot of floor space and offer very little, if any, storage space in return. As discussed earlier, a good pressing table height is just three inches higher than cutting height. This means that a lot of the choices discussed in the previous section for cutting tables are also good choices for pressing tables. The major difference is that a pressing surface shouldn't be deeper than 18". Irons are heavy, and you should not be reaching far from your body when manipulating one. In addition, the ideal pressing-surface width is long enough to accommodate fabric strips that are cut selvage to selvage (approximately 42" to 44").

If you decide to make your own pressing surface, you need to purchase or make a heat- and moisture-resistant surface on top. Several manufacturers make foldout cutting pads. Some ironing board cover manufacturers will make custom covers to fit your surface. You can also find the heat-resistant materials used in covers at fabric stores and online sources to make your own.

If you have limited floor space, ironing boards that store behind a cabinet door mounted into the wall may be your best bet. Then you can bring out your large ironing board only when needed and stow it quickly out of the way when it's not in use.

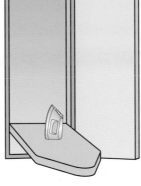

If you have a secondary pressing station by your sewing machine, you'll find that a large ironing board isn't needed all that often. But unless the board is easy to take out and put away, most quilters will find it more convenient to leave their board set up all the time. If this is the case, you might as well have a pressing surface that doubles as bulk storage.

If you are considering replacing your ironing board, make a graph paper model of your ideal pressing table for your room layout. I prefer a pressing surface size of approximately 54" x 18".

design wall

A design wall is an important feature of a quilter's studio that can take a lot of precious space. Most quilters I know use some form of batting or commercially available design wall tacked to their wall. Some quilters have made their own design walls by wrapping expanded polystyrene (EPS) insulation board (available at most hardware stores) or white foam board (available at art supply stores) with batting and attaching the whole assembly to the wall. This material allows quilters to pin directly into the design wall (like a bulletin board) without marring the wall underneath.

The size quilts you normally make will govern the size of the design wall you'll want to have in your studio. You could locate your design wall close to your sewing station so you can remove blocks from your wall without even getting up from your chair. Make an index-card paper model of your design wall to include in your graph paper layout.

storage solutions

Now that you have some ideas for improving the task-based portion of your studio, we can discuss storage needs. Fabric, books, works in progress, scraps, and patterns tend to require a lot of space. Each has its own unique requirements based on how you prefer to work.

fabric

By far the biggest storage problems I hear about from quilters concern fabric storage. Most quilters start with dresser drawers and boxes for fabric storage. Then, as their stash grows and they tire of digging through all of it in order to find something, they move it to clear plastic tubs. As the tubs become too heavy or too full to hold everything, some quilters graduate to rolling office carts. When the carts overflow or become too numerous, quilters move toward armoires, closet shelving, or bookcases. Sound familiar?

Most armoires and closets are too deep for good fabric storage. Aside from fat quarters, which are a whole other issue, the average quilter has between one and three yards of each piece of fabric in her stash. A 24"-deep shelf will cause you to stack your fabric double-deep or folded in such a way that you can't see a neat fabric edge at the front for each piece of fabric. A lot of bookshelves are too shallow (about 10" deep), causing fabric to hang off the front edge or requiring that it be folded excessively. However, if these bookcases have adjustable-height shelving, they are great for storing fabric bolts.

I recommend shelving that is between 14" and 16" deep for 1- to 3-yard cuts of flat-folded fabric. This allows you to fold your fabric in a standard way using a ruler or folding tool to set the width (for details, see "Fabric Folding" on page 28). Most upper kitchen cabinets are 12" deep, a bit shallow for flat-folded fabric. Most furniture units made to accommodate TVs aren't efficient for fabric storage because they are too deep. However, a lot of living room wall-unit shelving comes in 14" to 16" depths to accommodate stereo equipment, which is just the right size for folded fabric. And many glass-door curio cabinets meet the criteria.

Typically, bookcases aren't deep enough to store folded fabric efficiently, but if you can remove a shelf or two, they're perfect for housing fabric bolts.

FABRIC FOLDING

I prefer to use the Omnigrid 8½" x 24" ruler for folding any fabric that is greater than ½ yard (but less than 3 yards). First fold the fabric selvage to selvage (as it comes off the bolt). Then wrap the fabric around your ruler until it is all rolled up. Next slide the ruler halfway out of the fabric and fold the fabric in half. The folded fabric will be about 9" wide by 11" deep (depending on the quantity of fabric and the selvage-to-selvage size you started with). Stack these folded fabrics on the shelf so that only the last fold shows. You can fit four stacks side by side on 36"-wide shelves. Because fabric can be inconsistent in selvage-to-selvage measurements, just make sure that your folded front edges are even. No one will ever see the back edges when the fabrics are stacked on the shelf, so it's fine if the back edges are ragged.

If your shelves are 24" wide, you may wish to make a 7"-wide folding tool. Then you could have three stacks of fabric side by side on each shelf, for an efficient use of the space. I have successfully used heavy-duty cardboard, corrugated plastic, and foam board to make different folding tools. All work well, although they are not as sturdy as a ruler and they won't last indefinitely.

Fabric that is folded uniformly is easier to stack, creates a less cluttered appearance, and makes finding just the right fabric much easier.

Some bookcases may have deeper dimensions, too, but be sure to measure them before buying.

When shopping for furniture or shelving for fabric storage, take along your fabric-volume dimensions calculated from your existing stash. Take along a calculator too! Divide your calculated volume by 11" (the approximate depth of the fabric when it's folded using the technique described in the box, right).

In the armoire example on page 22, we calculated 41,040 cubic inches of storage space. About half of that space, or 20,500 cubic inches, was used to store quilt fabric; the rest was used to house batting, machine covers, and wool fabrics. To store 20,500 cubic inches of fabric, we would need a new cabinet with a frontal area (the height multiplied by the width) of roughly 1,900 square inches (20,500 divided by 11). If a cabinet is 74" tall, 30" wide, and more than 12" deep, it can hold 2,220 square inches of fabric (74 x 30 = 2,220). So, a cabinet this size will not only hold all the quilt fabrics in our example but also offer more than 300 square inches of extra space for future fabric purchases or for storing books.

As mentioned earlier, fabric will fade over time if it's exposed to sunlight or full-spectrum lighting. You may wish to consider solid doors instead of glass doors on your fabric cabinet to protect your investment from fading. Another good solution would be to locate open shelving in a walk-in closet with full-spectrum lighting that can be turned off when you are not looking for fabric. If you've selected wooden shelving, line the shelves with acid-free shelf paper to prevent wood oils or stain from transferring to your fabric. Whatever type of fabric storage you choose, try to locate it close to your cutting table or design space. This will allow you to easily audition new fabrics from your stash for any design you are working on.

books and magazines

Bookcases are the obvious answer for storing books and magazines. What is not obvious is that books need to be stored at eye level and need to be accessible from your design space. Public libraries and bookstores provide seating among the book-stacks so you can peruse the books while seated comfortably. Your books and magazines should be located wherever you will use them most. Magazines should be stored neatly in binders or magazine holders in order to stay upright on your shelves. It is often helpful to group books by style of quiltmaking or alphabetically by author.

Magazines can be sorted in any number of ways, but libraries usually store them by title and date for quick retrieval. Be aware that an easy trap to fall into is to save every issue of every magazine, regardless of whether you'll ever look at it again. You may wish to use a critical eye when deciding what to save. Fabrics and styles change rapidly. If you haven't consulted a particular book or magazine in a year, consider passing it along to someone else. It will free up space for you to bring new books and magazines into your quilting studio!

As you do when selecting fabric-storage furniture, keep your dimension requirements in mind when shopping for book and magazine shelving. If you are using the same shelving for both fabric and books, make sure you add their requirements together to determine the total storage volume required.

Store magazines in plastic or cardboard holders in your bookcase. You can generally store a year's worth of each subscription in one holder.

works in progress

Projects that have been started and are in various stages of completion can present a storage challenge. They range from a collection of blocks to bags of coordinating fabrics, thread, patterns, embellishments, and sometimes books or magazines, to whole quilt tops or partially quilted quilts.

Baskets, shoe boxes, or plastic bins are often used to store WIP. These are fine for short-term storage but have some disadvantages too. Plastic tubs do not allow airflow, and fabric stored in them for long periods of time will mold due to the inherent moisture in the natural cotton fibers. Shoe boxes come in many sizes and can look chaotic when stacked on a shelf. I prefer newly purchased pizza or meat-patty boxes available from cardboard suppliers. Most have white exteriors and locking tabs to keep small items like buttons or thread from falling out. The boxes can sit vertically or horizontally on standard-depth shelving, making efficient use of space. I like to cover them with fabric, using fusible web to hold it in place.

Divided baskets are a good way to organize fat quarters and scraps.

Covered in decorative fabric or left plain, flat boxes are an efficient way to store works in progress.

"...joyful always."

Use a ruler rack or basket to contain and organize your rulers, or hang them on your cutting table for easy access.

If you are using cardboard boxes for long-term storage, I recommend lining them with acid-free paper. Cardboard can break down over time and discolor fabric that is in contact with it. Also, cardboard needs to be stored indoors and away from areas with high humidity such as basements or unheated attics.

Finished quilt tops or partially quilted quilts store best on 24"-deep shelving. Use acid-free paper in the folds and keep your WIP out of sunlight or full-spectrum light to reduce fading.

Just as with other storage needs, if you intend to use shelving to hold WIP, you will need to know volume requirements to calculate shelving needs. Since you will not be accessing these items every day, store WIP boxes and partially finished tops on the highest or lowest shelves. Be aware that if they're stored too far out of sight, you may forget that you have them and never finish them.

other storage needs

Be sure to include extra drawer and shelf space in your design solutions for storage of smaller items such as fat quarters, scraps, patterns, and tools.

Fat quarters. Smaller cuts of fabric, such as fat quarters and 1/3-yard or 1/2-yard pieces, present their own challenge for storage and retrieval. They need a different folding method than larger pieces of fabric and work well in drawers or baskets rather than stacked on shelves. You'll need drawers or containers about 5" to 6" deep to hold fat quarters and 1/2-yard cuts of fabric neatly.

Scraps. The best way to store scraps depends on what you intend to do with them. If you never make scrappy quilts or small appliqué blocks, then you may want to donate your scraps to someone who does. If your scraps just keep growing until they fill multiple large trash bags, think about why you are saving them in the first place. They are certainly inaccessible and taking up large amounts of space for the value they add. If, on the other hand, you frequently use scraps and need them to be accessible, you may need a scrap plan.

What is a scrap plan? It is a consistent way of dealing with leftover fabric from any project so that you can find the scraps you need when you need them. I've heard many methods discussed

FAT QUARTER FOLDING

Many fabric stores often have their own unique way of folding fat quarters. I prefer to use the Omnigrid 4" x 14" ruler to fold my fat quarters consistently. I begin by folding the fat quarter in half, selvage to cut edge. Then I lay my ruler across the end of the adjacent cut edge and wrap the fabric around the ruler until the fabric is completely rolled up. Next I slide the ruler halfway out of the fabric roll and fold the wrap in half. Your finished fabric pack should be a rectangle close to 4½" x 5½". This will store neatly stacked on shallow shelving, or upright in 6" deep drawers or storage boxes. This same method will work for ¼-yard to ½-yard fabric cuts. You may want to put smaller pieces in your scrap basket.

by quilters who make scrappy quilts. Some cut all fabric that is less than 1/4 yard into strips of standard widths or blocks of standard sizes and store the pieces sorted by value (light, medium, and dark). Some keep all scraps, regardless of size, and sort them by color into boxes. Others throw away scraps that are less than a certain size. And there are those who dig through the trash at quilt retreats to keep even the smallest trimmings! Whatever your preference, make a conscious choice to handle scraps before they get out of control. You're more likely to use your scraps in future projects if you can easily locate what you have.

Patterns. Quilt patterns can be slipped into clear sheet protectors and stored in notebooks. Or they can be stored in office file drawers, shoe boxes, or magazine organizers. If you prefer to consult your patterns during the design phase of a project, store them at eye level within easy reach of your design area.

Tools. I cannot stress enough how important it is to store your tools where you need them. Cutting tools at the cutting station, pressing tools at the pressing station, and sewing tools at the sewing station are all a good start for tool storage. There are thousands of products on the market made to store tools and supplies. Office-supply storage, kitchen storage, garage storage, and even bathroom organizers can all be considered for use in the quilting studio. I personally prefer multiple drawers in each area to store the majority of tools and supplies out of sight. A clutter-free surface makes it easier for me to work. I don't care for pegboards, because they create a lot of visual clutter.

Several sewing notions suppliers sell ruler organizers that either rest on the cutting surface or hang on the wall. If you have the wall space, the hanging variety will keep your cutting surface clutter free. If you already have a ruler rack or basket that rests on the cutting surface, you can build a small shelf attached to the wall a few inches above your cutting table to accommodate your tools and keep your surface cleared. Another simple solution to ruler storage is to put small nails in your wall or the side of your cutting table to hang your rulers out of the way.

I am frequently amazed by the number of notions that are stored on sewing tables. Obviously these items are out because they're used frequently while machine piecing or quilting. Personally, I prefer my sewing table to remain clear of notions when I'm not sewing. A simple solution is to use an organizer to help corral the most frequently used sewing notions at the end of the day. If your sewing table is positioned against a wall, an inexpensive solution is to hang a small shelf a few inches above your sewing table to hold baskets, cups, and tins of your high-use notions.

shop without buying

At this point you may know enough about your major furniture needs to go shopping, but don't buy anything yet! You'll want to read "Turning Your Design into Reality" on page 34 before purchasing anything new. You know the ideal height and size of sewing, cutting, and pressing surfaces for your body. And you know what your fabric-storage requirements are. Now start auditioning furniture on your graph paper layout of your quilting studio. Cut out scale paper models of possible new furniture pieces and move them around your studio. Window shop online or in catalogs from office-furniture supply

stores and ready-to-assemble (RTA) furniture sources. Use their dimensions to make models of possible furniture solutions (keep a list of sources and prices). As you move the models around, keep in mind traffic flow from doorways including the door-swing space. Interior design rules apply here:

- Walkways between furniture should be 36" or wider.
- Leave room for chairs to slide in and out.
- Don't block doorways or heat registers.

Design walls work well located behind doors, because they don't interfere with the door swing. Sewing and cutting tables work well located under windows, since you won't be able to reach very high above the sewing table for ergonomically safe retrieval of heavier stored items. Closets are best used for bulk storage of large items. Portable cutting or pressing tables on wheels can be in front of a design wall, because they can be rolled out of the way when you want to use the entire design space. Use as much vertical space as possible when picking solutions. Floor space is often very precious, so the higher you go up the wall (and can still comfortably reach), the more floor space you will free up. Check the height of storage units against your ceiling height to make sure they will fit.

play, play, play

You will need to spend some time playing with your paper models to create possible layouts. I try to create up to 10 viable layout options, and I use a digital camera to preserve them all for comparison purposes.

It's really important that you spend the time to find a solution that you absolutely love. Your solution needs to incorporate the best ergonomics, work triangle, and storage for your needs. After you have settled on a quilt studio design that meets your needs, tape your furniture pieces in place. This will be your working layout for the next phase of your makeover—turning your design into a reality!

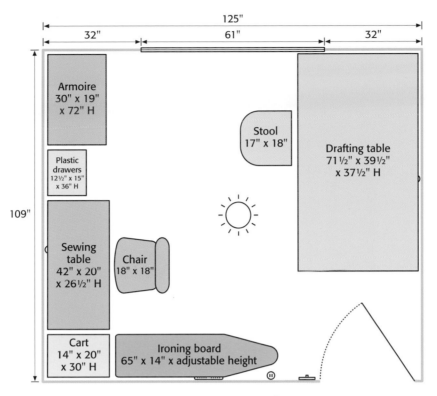

Plan view with existing furniture

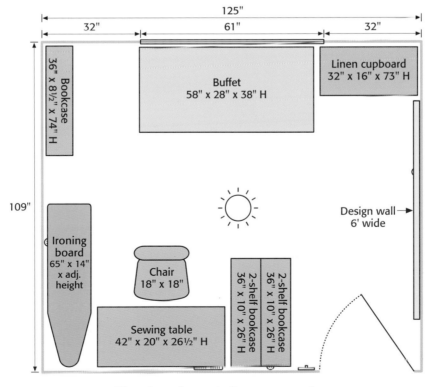

Plan view of new studio arrangement

turning your design into reality

AFTER YOU'VE SELECTED YOUR FURNITURE and settled on a design for your new quilting studio, you need to use your project-management skills to make it happen. You may wish to draw elevation views of your walls to get a perspective on what your final studio design will look like. (An elevation view is simply the view of each wall from floor to ceiling rather than the overhead or bird's-eye view of the initial plan). You can use it to show the planned location of all your fabric, books, and magazines, and to verify that everything will fit. It is also helpful in communicating with contractors or your spouse as well as for visualizing your finished room.

It's helpful to make a spreadsheet of your budget and actual costs so you'll know if you're on track. You may also want to make a schedule of the activities that need to happen. This chapter will help you with the basic steps of creating your perfect quilting space.

drawing an elevation view

An elevation view can show you what each wall will look like after furniture is installed. Using your room measurements, draw a scale layout of each wall on ¼" graph paper. Using your furniture heights and widths, draw scale models of the furniture located against each wall to show all four walls of a quilt studio. Measure shelf heights and pencil in shelf locations (even if they are behind cabinet doors). Make sure light switches, electrical outlets, and heat registers are accessible. Consider moving outlets or relocating furniture if they are blocking access. Map your supplies into their final locations on the elevation views. Add labels to your elevation view to show a plan for locating fabric, books, magazines, works in progress, scraps, tools, and supplies. Use your room and furniture dimensions along with storage volumes from page 21 to ensure that your final design will accommodate all the contents of your quilt studio.

budget spreadsheet

It is really helpful to create a basic list of the work you need to do and the costs associated with that work. A sample budget worksheet is shown on page 37, and a blank worksheet is provided on page 40 for you to photocopy and use. Simply leave blank the portions that don't apply. For each item,

write the word *keep* for the items you plan to reuse in your new studio. For items you'll be replacing, write the description, name of the store where you'll buy it, and estimated cost.

If during this process you find that your dream studio is exceeding your budget, go back to your self assessment (see pages 18–22) and go over the prioritized list of your needs. Again, I encourage you to consider ergonomics as your first priority. A comfortable and injury-free experience should be the first and fore-most consideration in making a productive quilter's studio. Next, I recommend that you focus on layout of your space, making U-shaped workstations for sewing, even if you do not replace your furniture. Finally, focus on efficient storage for the items that take up the most volume in your studio, which most likely will be fabric.

Due to possible budget constraints, you may need to take a phased approach to creating your perfect studio. Phase one might be improving

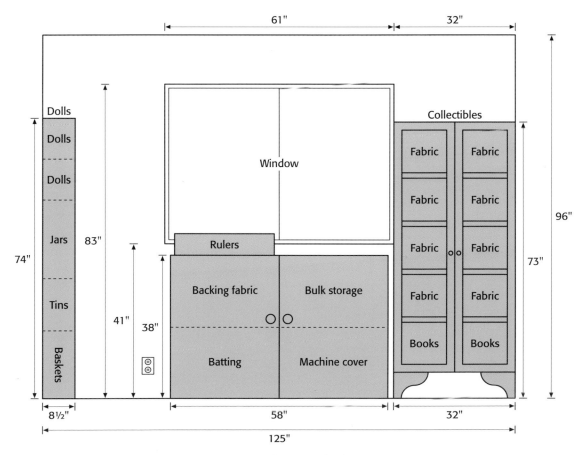

Elevation view of new studio design

Mapping storage into the elevation view of your room ensures that everything will fit in your new studio.

ergonomics only. After you have recovered financially from phase one, you may wish to do phase two, which would address storage solutions.

After you have locked in on your furniture choices and completed your working budget, make a schedule for your makeover.

schedule

A schedule is simply a list of the work you intend to do in sequence with the appropriate time allotted for each task. I like using software-based programs like Microsoft Project to make my schedules, but this is overkill for most do-it-yourselfers. Another option is to use a blank calendar page and jot down the tasks on the dates you think you can do them. You'll find a sample makeover schedule on page 38 that you can use as a guide.

Each task needs a beginning date and an ending date. Be realistic about selecting dates. If you work full time, don't expect to get huge amounts of work done on weeknights. If you know you are going out of town, don't schedule work to be done while you're gone unless you have a spouse or contractors that will continue in your absence.

let's go!

Now that you have a plan, a budget, and a schedule that meet your needs, you are ready to go. As in any home-remodeling project, you may not get much else done during the next few weeks. Try to focus your energy on your quilt studio and remember that the gains will far outweigh the pain!

Step 1: Photograph. Take pictures of your studio, including all four walls. You'll love comparing these "before" photos with the fabulous "after" photos of your makeover.

Step 2: Pack up and move out. Depending on how invasive your remodel will be, you may need to pack up the contents of your quilt studio and move out to a temporary sewing space during the remodel. If you are ordering furniture with a long lead time, it's a good idea to place that order now.

Step 3: Make electrical and lighting changes. Since most electrical work requires cutting into walls, this work needs to happen first. Be sure that a qualified electrician handles all electrical modifications.

Verify with your electrician that you have an adequate number of outlets that are accessible at the sewing, cutting, and pressing stations. Be aware that irons draw a lot of power (500–1000 watts), and multiple irons on a circuit may blow the breaker. Sometimes even a single iron on the same circuit with lighting will cause the lighting to flicker as the iron cycles through its heating phase. The same goes for window-unit air conditioners. If you have one planned for your space, consider adding a separate circuit for it.

If you're having new lighting installed, it should be done at the same time that any other electrical changes are made.

Step 4: Paint walls. Since you have your room completely cleaned out, now is a perfect time to add a fresh coat of paint. Keep in mind that dark colors tend to absorb light, making a room seem darker, while light colors reflect light, making the room seem brighter.

Step 5: Install flooring. Many quilters prefer hard floors for rolling their sewing chairs around

Sample Budget Worksheet

Category	Item	Description	Source	Budget	Actual Cost	Saved (Overspent)
Room Changes	Lighting	Garage sale lamp	Garage sale	$50	$2	$48
	Painting	Supplies and paint—in stock	Hardware store	$50	$30	$20
	Flooring	New laminate—1 week lead time	Hardware store	$500	$450	$50
	Sewing table—primary	Keep	N/A	$0	$0	$0
	Sewing table—secondary	Not needed	N/A	$0	$0	$0
	Cutting table—primary	Buffet—in stock	Designer's Warehouse	$300	$162	$138
	Cutting table—secondary	Build top on bookcases	Make	$50	$25	$25
Furniture Options	Pressing surface—primary	Keep	N/A	$0	$0	$0
	Pressing surface—secondary	Keep	N/A	$0	$0	$0
	Chair	Keep	N/A	$0	$0	$0
	Computer desk	Not needed	N/A	$0	$0	$0
	Fabric	Martha Linen Cupboard—4 weeks lead time	The Bramble Company	$500	$325	$175
	Books	Same as fabric storage	N/A	$0	$0	$0
	Magazines	Same as fabric storage	N/A	$0	$0	$0
	Patterns	Same as fabric storage	N/A	$0	$0	$0
	Tools	Ruler rack and notions boxes	Quilt store and Ikea	$75	$75	$0
	WIP	White boxes	Clearview Designs	$50	$20	$30
Organize	Design wall	Expanded polystyrene (EPS) with batting cover	Make	$50	$35	$15
	Raggedy Anns	Bookshelf	Garage sale	$30	$15	$15
	Bears	Same as fabric storage	N/A	$0	$0	$0
	Vintage clothing	Keep	N/A	$0	$0	$0
Total				$1,655	$1,139	$516

October

Monday	Tuesday	Wednesday	Thursday	Friday	Sat/Sun
		1 Take a picture SELF ASSESSMENT – Measure everything – Draw layout – Make paper dolls – Calculate volumes	**2**	**3** Play with layouts	**4** **5**
6 SHOPPING w/o BUYING	**7**	**8**	**9** Play with layouts (again) – Choose best	**10** PLAN – Draw elevations – Make budget sheet – Schedule – Order furniture & supplies	**11** Pack up & move out **12**
13 ELECTRICAL & LIGHTING	**14** Patch walls	**15** PAINTING	**16**	**17** FLOORING	**18** **19**
20 ASSEMBLE & INSTALL FURNITURE	**21**	**22** Make pressing surface	**23** Make design wall	**24** Fold fabric & put away Sort books & magazines	**25** **26**
27 Buy organizers for notions, WIP, & tools	**28** Put notions, WIP, & tools away	**29** Take a picture & ENJOY!	**30**	**31**	

Sample makeover schedule

between workstations. They also find that it's easier to dust mop threads from hard floors than to vacuum them from carpets. If you have or choose a floor such as hardwood or vinyl, place a small carpet with a pad under it by your cutting station to reduce fatigue while standing. Other quilters like carpeting for its cushioning capability and use office mats for ease of rolling their chairs while seated.

In either case, if you are changing flooring, you need to do it next. Several of the makeovers in this book feature hardwood laminates as the flooring choice. In other makeovers, the quilters were content to keep their original carpeted floors.

Step 6: Buy, assemble, or build furniture. A lot of the furniture choices for the remodels in this book are RTA (ready to assemble). These items come in flat boxes and require very little knowledge, tools, or mechanical ability to assemble. Don't feel intimidated by furniture that requires assembly. Quilters generally have good spatial skills and know how to read a pattern, whether it is for sewing or furniture assembly. These pieces can be heavy and awkward to manipulate by yourself during assembly, but most retailers of RTA furniture offer delivery and assembly services for a fee.

If your plan includes custom-built cabinetry, use your layout and elevation drawings to communicate your needs specifically. Be sure the cabinetmaker understands the important dimensions for ergonomics and storage.

Step 7: Sort and fold. As you unpack your boxes of fabric, decide what to keep and what to give away. Sort by color or fabric family such as batiks or 1930s reproductions. If the fabric is less than ¼ yard, consider putting it with your scraps. Fold your fabric and place it on shelves or in drawers per your plan.

Sort your scraps into baskets, bins, or boxes by color or size. Locate your scrap storage near your cutting table to make it easier to sort as you are making the scraps in the first place. If you have a lot of scraps but you rarely use them, you may wish to store them in a closet or under a bed. There's no need to use precious quilt-studio space for items that are not used every day.

Sort your books, patterns, and magazines. Buy magazine holders or notebooks for magazines. Buy notebooks or boxes, or recycle shoe boxes for patterns. Label holders, notebooks, and boxes with their contents to make retrieval easier.

Step 8: Store tools. Install ruler racks, nails for hanging rulers, and shelves for holding supplies; place baskets of supplies near where they are needed. For each tool, think "Where will I be when I need this most often?" and store the item within easy reach of that location. Put the majority of items in drawers, baskets, or boxes to reduce visual clutter. Keep out only the most necessary daily-use items: your favorite ruler and cutter at your cutting station, and a seam ripper and scissors at your sewing station. Store rarely used items on the highest shelves or in bottom drawers.

Step 9: Store works in progress. Sort unfinished objects into two piles: projects you love and will finish someday, and projects you're no longer crazy about and should donate to someone else. Then come up with an organized way to store WIP or UFOs. It will give your quilt studio a less cluttered appearance. Label each box with a picture, name, or piece of fabric to indicate its contents.

Step 10: Test-drive your studio. Sit at your sewing station and try out your secondary cutting and pressing surfaces. Open drawers and reach for tools and supplies needed for sewing. Sew an inaugural quilt block. Move supplies and tools if they are not conveniently located. Stand at your cutting station and cut some strips. Press your block and look around for things you may need while pressing. Check locations against your plan. Rearrange the fabric and supplies that you use most often to the shelves and drawers that are easiest to see and reach. Test-drive your entire space while thinking about ergonomics and efficiency.

Step 11: Photograph your finished studio. Congratulations! You have successfully transformed your quilting space into an ergonomic, efficient, and organized studio. Take pictures to show your quilting friends.

Budget Worksheet

Category	Item	Description	Source	Budget	Actual Cost	Saved (Overspent)
Room Changes						
Furniture Options						
Organize						
	Total					

real-life quilt studio makeovers

EACH QUILTER HAS A UNIQUE STYLE in designing and creating quilts. In addition, each room or setting has unique limitations that drive different solutions in designing the perfect quilt studio. The seven examples in this chapter will introduce you to eight different quilters and their specific needs. The makeovers increase in complexity and cost from the first one to the last one.

As you read each example, think about your quilt studio and keep a list of things you like about each one. This may help you decide which solutions you would like to incorporate into your studio. Look for similarities to your studio in size and in door, window, and closet layout.

rearranging what you already own

BEFORE THE MAKEOVER, I could only sew during my kids' naps, after my husband got home from work, or when the kids were in bed. Now, after relocating my creative space near the kitchen area, I can bake or cook and sew at the same time. While the chicken is browning, I can sew a few strips together! —*Jayna Hammericksen*

the situation

Jayna is a young stay-at-home mom of two preschoolers. She was excited about quilting but finding it hard to fit a few minutes for her craft into her day.

- Jayna did not have an extra room in her house for quilting. She managed to squeeze a sewing table into the master bedroom, along with a folding card table for cutting. But when the sewing table was open, it blocked the closet door. Jayna did her pressing on the master bathroom counter using a pressing pad. Her fabric was stored in plastic bins stacked in the corner of the bedroom, with larger bulk-storage items kept in the garage.

before

43

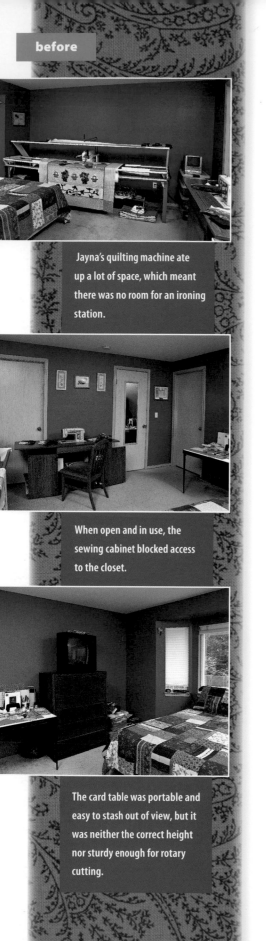

Jayna's quilting machine ate up a lot of space, which meant there was no room for an ironing station.

When open and in use, the sewing cabinet blocked access to the closet.

The card table was portable and easy to stash out of view, but it was neither the correct height nor sturdy enough for rotary cutting.

- Jayna received a wonderful gift from her husband's parents: a quilting machine! She managed to shoehorn the machine into the master bedroom with her other quilting items.

- Not only did the bedroom lack space, it was simply located too far from the center of household activity. Jayna could see the kids in the backyard through the upstairs bedroom window, but she had to travel the full length of the house to get out the back door to where they were playing.

- When the kids were indoors in the family room, she couldn't hear or see them because she was at the opposite end of the house. Jayna found that the only time she had for quilting was when the kids were napping.

- Jayna had to clean up after each sewing session, so as not to clutter up the bedroom.

- Lastly, there was simply no room for a design wall in the bedroom.

the solutions

Jayna needed some quick fixes for ergonomics and storage while we worked on a more extensive yet inexpensive solution. It was obvious to me that we needed to move her quilting out of the master bedroom.

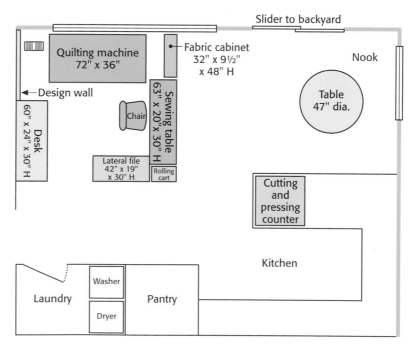

Jayna's new quilt studio layout

The kitchen peninsula is the perfect height for rotary cutting, and it's conveniently located by the fabric cabinet (shown at left in background).

A vintage cabinet recycled from the garage now displays neatly folded fabric and baskets for tools and scraps.

raise the cutting table height

The card table that Jayna used for cutting was shorter than 30" high, much too low for a cutting surface for a woman of average height. An immediate solution was to use leg extenders. These adjustable-height extenders are useful on straight-leg tables of any size.

increase storage

Another quick solution for Jayna was using bed risers to increase the height of the under-bed storage area. Risers provide 5" to 10" more inches of space, so now Jayna can place her fabric-storage bins under her bed, freeing up space for an ironing surface in her room. These small changes helped Jayna immediately while we were planning her complete studio makeover.

relocate to a more practical space

Moving Jayna to a more centralized location in her house seemed to be a perfect solution, providing that her children's safety (keeping them away from her machines and cutters) could be addressed. Jayna's house had a bright, sunny kitchen with an oversized eating

nook and sliding doors to the patio. The large windows and high ceiling just begged for the space to become a quilt studio. The main pieces of furniture in the oversized nook were the dining table and the computer desk. We moved her existing sewing furniture into her nook, using the furniture to block the area off from the rest of the room. A child's gate at the one entrance to her area allowed Jayna to leave out partially finished projects without worrying about little hands getting stuck with pins or finding sharp rotary cutters.

take advantage of space to multitask

From Jayna's new location, she could easily watch the kids in the backyard, help them with snacks at the kitchen table, and hear them next door in the family room. Close proximity to the kitchen also allowed her to multitask with meal preparation. The laundry room was right next to the quilting space, allowing her to easily wash fabric or keep tabs on household laundry. Having the computer nearby, she was able to work on email with guild members and track family finances in between steps of quilting.

additional benefits

Beyond the immediate benefits of putting Jayna in the center of her household, we improved her ergonomics and storage issues.

- Jayna discovered that her large kitchen breakfast bar was the ideal height for cutting fabric—plus it was too high for the kids to reach. The lighting at the kitchen counter was excellent for cutting by day or night. A trade-off was that fabric and cutting supplies always had to be cleaned up before food prep could begin.

- Jayna's fabric is much more visible and accessible in her new studio. We displayed folded fabric in a glass-door cabinet that she had in storage. Her books and magazines

were moved from a hall closet to the computer hutch. She archived some family files from the computer desk drawers and lateral file to free up space for sewing notions and supplies. There was even enough wall space to sport a design wall next to the computer desk.

- Finally, we placed the lateral file next to her sewing table to make an L-shaped workstation so she can press or trim blocks while seated at her sewing station. This surface is accessible to the kids, so she needs to be careful that a hot iron or rotary cutter isn't left unattended.

the bottom line

By rearranging existing furniture and borrowing furniture from other uses, we were able to produce Jayna's dream quilting space in a different location within her house.

Total cost: less than $100

Where the money went: design wall, cutting-and-pressing pad

Lessons learned: Take a close look at the furniture in your house. Do you have furniture that is being underutilized that you could borrow for your quilt studio? Bookcases, bedroom dressers, curio cabinets, and computer desks are all great items to call into duty for your quilt studio.

bargain shopping

I LOVE LOOKING AT MY FABRICS and project box organizers. And I especially love the way my design wall works! —*Michele Williams*

the situation

Michele recently started her own antiques business, and her interest in antiques and collectibles was very evident in her quilt studio. She displayed her Raggedy Ann and teddy bear collections along with antique baby-christening gowns in her studio. It was important to Michele that these items stay a part of her new studio.

- With no closet and an extra small (9' x 10') room, Michele had a serious lack of storage space.

- The dominant feature of her quilt studio was an enormous antique drafting table. It was exactly the right height for cutting, and Michele loved it. But the table took up one-third of the room's usable floor space and offered little in the way of underneath storage. As we all do when faced with storage issues, Michele had tucked boxes and bags of fabric and supplies under the table. She had to crawl under the table and dig out the items she needed and then stack them back in when she was done.

before

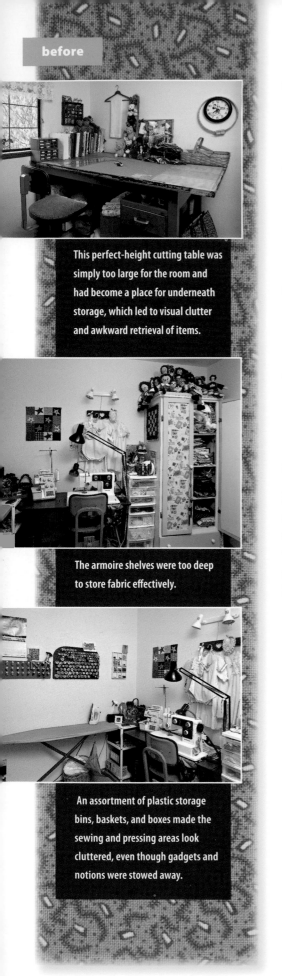

This perfect-height cutting table was simply too large for the room and had become a place for underneath storage, which led to visual clutter and awkward retrieval of items.

The armoire shelves were too deep to store fabric effectively.

An assortment of plastic storage bins, baskets, and boxes made the sewing and pressing areas look cluttered, even though gadgets and notions were stowed away.

- Michele's large drafting table afforded her a huge work surface when needed. But as is typical when using too large a surface, the drafting table became a permanent storage location for everything that didn't have another home.

- While Michele's armoire kept her fabric dust free and protected it from UV light, the armoire wasn't the right solution for her needs. She had collected many small pieces of fabric and scraps. The armoire was so deep that Michele had been stacking fabric in two rows, one behind the other. She couldn't see all her fabric at once and had to dig out the front row to get to the fabric in the back.

- Given that the wall behind the drafting table was unreachable, and the window, door, and armoire took up a good portion of the three other walls, there wasn't much space left for a design wall—a feature Michele named as her highest priority in her new studio.

- Michele didn't care for the carpeting in her room because she is sensitive to dust, and she wanted to be able to roll her chair easily across the floor.

the solutions

Michele was on a tight budget, so we needed creative, low-cost solutions. Her makeover was a real challenge due to double constraints—space and budget. We settled on a desired layout for her room before we had the exact furniture pieces that met her needs. We auditioned many furniture solutions over the course of several months. And because Michele is a savvy shopper, she was able to save herself a lot of money.

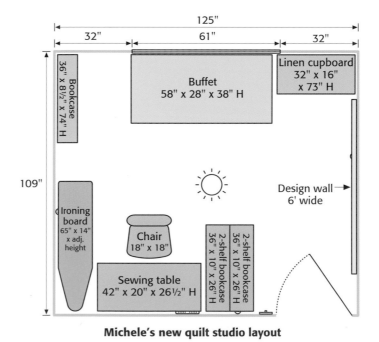

Michele's new quilt studio layout

find the right furniture at the right price

Armed with her calculated dimensions, Michele bought a new cutting table from a furniture store that was going out of business. Then she found her fabric-storage unit at a discount furniture importer and waited months for its arrival from the Far East. She found her display bookcase and lighting through savvy garage-sale shopping.

increase surface area with a creative extension

Michele's new cutting table is a buffet cabinet with doors and pullout shelving. Her husband, Brian, added a 10"-deep extension on the back of her buffet surface to make it the appropriate depth for her cutting mat and tools. The new surface area is equal to the usable surface area of her old drafting table, but it provides easier-to-access storage underneath.

create a secondary cutting area that doubles as storage

An inexpensive and creative solution that we incorporated into her studio is a secondary cutting area. When Michele is seated at her sewing machine, she has a complete U-shaped workstation. Her vintage ironing board is on the right side for pressing, and a newly made storage area with a cutting station on top is on the left. The cutting station is made from two small bookcases, which Michele already owned, placed back to back and topped with a homemade plywood surface. The bookcase

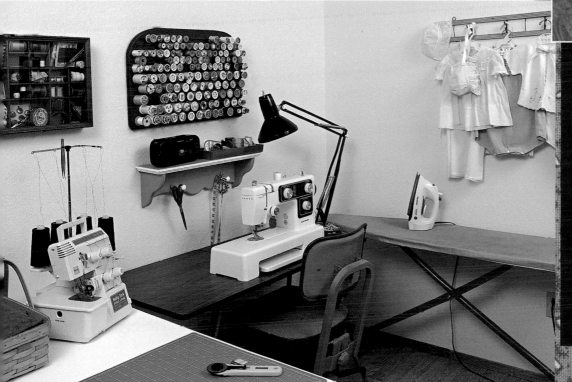

Above: Inexpensive bookcases placed back to back are perfect for storing boxes of WIP and notions. Add a plywood top for a handy cutting surface.

Left: The bookcase topper (foreground) allows for a secondary cutting station as well as a spot for Michele's serger. Since this station is right by the door, it's also a handy place for the basket she takes along to quilt guild meetings.

Moving the cutting station below the window freed up the large wall by the door for use as a design wall. The cutting table is smaller but affords much better underneath storage, which is concealed by doors. Now it's the perfect place for hiding batting, machine covers, and other bulky items.

facing the door contains her project boxes. Michele wanted to see her UFOs every time she entered her studio to increase her likelihood of completing these works in progress.

The other bookcase faces the sewing space—perfect for supplies and notion storage. I love drawers for this kind of storage, but an inexpensive alternative is using multiple boxes with the contents sorted, organized, and labeled. Michele has a lot of lace, ribbon, elastic, buttons, rickrack and other assorted supplies, but she had outgrown her stack of plastic drawers for these items. The new boxes are tidy, and they allow her to find what she needs without getting up from her sewing area.

create a low-cost design wall

Brian also built her design wall, situating it on the wall behind the door swing. This makes perfect sense, because it is very low profile and takes up no floor space. When open, the door covers only a small portion of the design wall, and the door can be closed when the whole design wall is needed.

Michele's design wall is made from 4' x 8' sheets of 1"-thick expanded polystyrene (EPS) wrapped in cotton batting, which is then pinned in place with hatpins. The design wall serves double duty, also acting as a bulletin board. She can clean it with a simple lint roller or easily replace the cover when it becomes too dirty.

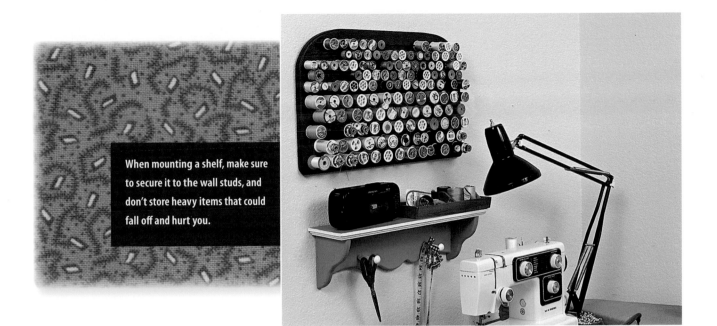

When mounting a shelf, make sure to secure it to the wall studs, and don't store heavy items that could fall off and hurt you.

additional benefits

In addition to a room with great storage, it was important to Michele to have the things she needed visible. She also enjoyed seeing her favorite collections while working in her studio.

- We added a shelf just above and behind Michele's sewing machine to help keep the sewing table completely clean.

- During her weeks of bargain shopping, Michele found a bookcase with 8½" deep shelving at a garage sale. It was too shallow for fabric or books, but it worked very well to display her Raggedy Ann dolls, wooden spools, antique tins, and basket collections. Grouping the collectibles together makes them a focal point of the room.

the bottom line

Michele is a savvy shopper who invested a lot of time searching for just the right furniture pieces. She saved herself more money by doing a lot of the work herself. She painted the room and worked alongside her husband to install new laminate flooring.

Total cost: less than $1,200

Where the money went: laminate flooring (approximately $400); furniture (about $500); storage supplies, paint, and building materials ($300)

Lessons learned: Like Michele, you can shop at garage sales, thrift stores, and furniture liquidators with your ideal furniture dimensions in hand. Bring your linear inches of books or volume of fabric to ensure that your new furniture piece will actually hold what you need to store; these purchases generally can't be returned. It's handy to bring paint chips and wood or fabric samples, too, if you need to match existing furniture or decor, and always keep storage potential in mind.

reducing visual clutter

I LOVE THE OVERALL NEAT AND TIDY APPEARANCE of my room with the new shelves. All the clutter is behind doors now or in semi-transparent bins. I ended up with lots more storage space also, so I have been having fun buying more books, fabrics, and tools to fill it all up again!—*Shannon Carnardo*

the situation

Shannon is at a stage in her life where she has more time for quilting because her kids are young adults. She is very resourceful and enjoyed keeping an organized studio in an upstairs bedroom. She explained to me that her studio was her oasis. Shannon spends a lot of time in her studio; she enjoys a morning cup of tea there before leaving for work, and she even watches television and movies in her room while sewing. Frankly, she liked her quilt studio, and wasn't sure it was really in need of a makeover.

before

Large bins of fabric were too heavy to reach from upper shelves, and the ironing board hindered easy access to most of what was stored there.

The design wall was freestanding, which meant it took up valuable floor space in this room. Also, because it was behind the cutting table, the bottom portion of the design wall was inaccessible.

Books were stored neatly but inefficiently on built-in shelves in the closet—all the storage space in front of them was wasted.

- The cutting table was partially blocking the path from the door into the room. Shannon had to be careful that she didn't run into the sharp corner of the table when passing through the door in a hurry.

- Both her sewing and embroidery machines were set up at all times in her quilt studio, but because their locations weren't conveniently close to one another, she used a separate chair for each workstation.

- Shannon's books were stored in her closet behind the sliding doors on a built-in shelving unit. The wonderful, deep, bulk-storage capacity of the closet was being wasted on books, which store easily on much shallower shelves.

- Shannon had some great modular shelving that she used for storing her plastic bins of fabric. But she had trouble accessing the bins because her ironing board stood in front of the shelving.

- Her design wall was made from a modular partition wall covered in batting. It took up about 14" of floor space, because it had to be leaned against the wall to keep it from falling over.

the solutions

The layout we chose for Shannon's studio opened up her floor space and made her room feel more spacious.

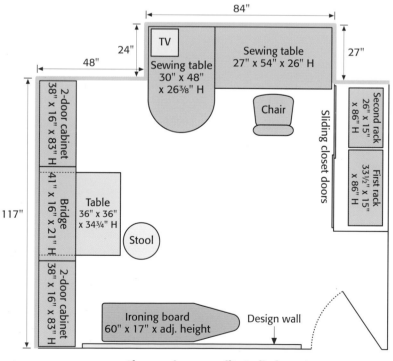

Shannon's new quilt studio layout

add storage wall to reduce clutter

To increase Shannon's overall storage capability and reduce visual clutter, we put in a wall of storage as a focal point for the room. The storage units are designed to flank a television stand with a bridge over the top. Shannon bought everything but the television stand and used the unit to bridge her existing cutting table. We added an under-cabinet lighting bar to improve her visibility so she can cut without casting shadows.

use deep shelving to take advantage of closet space

To take full advantage of her deep closet, the shallow closet shelving was replaced with the deep modular shelving that she had been using elsewhere in her studio. Shannon liked having her fabric in plastic bins, so we just moved the bins into one side of her closet. That way she could access all her fabric at once. The larger fabric bins are extremely heavy, so we put them on the easiest-to-reach shelves.

before

A new L-shaped sewing setup accommodates both machines, while a roll-out cart can be called into duty as a small cutting surface to form a U-shaped workstation.

combine workstations into U-shaped sewing space

Both machines are set up and accessible from one chair, and Shannon can easily roll her chair around to access her laptop computer, which holds her downloadable embroidery designs (see page 54).

move threads, notions, and supplies within easy reach

Shannon has a small cutting mat on top of her rolling notions cart that she can use for block trimming while seated. All of her threads and machine supplies are located in the closet next to her, so they're within easy reach from her chair.

incorporate space for collections and personal touches

All of Shannon's books, magazines, and patterns are stored at eye level in one cabinet, and the opposite cabinet is filled with more plastic bins of craft supplies. With all the storage bins tucked neatly behind doors, Shannon can use the display space above the cabinets and on the bridge-unit shelves for showcasing her handmade baskets and other collectibles. The drawers in the storage units are a great place to store extra supplies and notions.

additional benefits

- Another space-saving idea was to perch Shannon's television on a wall bracket so she can glance at it while sewing. Now it doesn't take up valuable floor or counter space.

- The area where Shannon's cutting table used to be now has a design wall mounted on the wall with the ironing board in front. The ironing board has a shallower profile than the cutting table, so it doesn't block the pathway from the door.

the bottom line

Most of Shannon's makeover budget was spent on furniture.

Total cost: about $1,000

Where the money went: two storage cabinets, a new sewing table, a TV bracket, some lights, design wall hardware and materials

Lessons learned: The design solution that we came up with for Shannon incorporates some of the same features as other design solutions. We reduced visual clutter by putting everything behind solid-door cabinets or closet doors. We gave her room a more open feel by moving furniture away from the doorway. Finally, we gave her a single U-shaped workstation that gave her easy access to both of her sewing machines.

going vertical

I LOVE MY NEW STORAGE SPACE. Besides there being a place for everything, my cabinets are gorgeous. One of my favorite relaxation techniques is to open my cabinet doors and the drawers where my fat quarters are lovingly folded and waiting, and recline in my new armchair to admire my abundant stash.—*Julie Wood*

the situation

Julie is a busy working mom of four children. She had sewed clothing and crafts for many years prior to getting bitten by the quilting bug. When quilting took over the majority of her spare time, she became interested in making a permanent home for her sewing machine. Julie had already learned the lesson of "location promotes productivity" and had planted her quilting studio in the busiest hub of her house. After years of camping on the dining table and having to clean up whenever the family needed the table for a meal together, Julie took over a portion of the family room for her sewing area.

• Julie started off with a simple office table and some heavy-duty garage cabinets. This worked for a while, but soon the need for an organizing plan was apparent. Julie's fabric was overflowing the industrial cabinets into other rooms of the house.

before

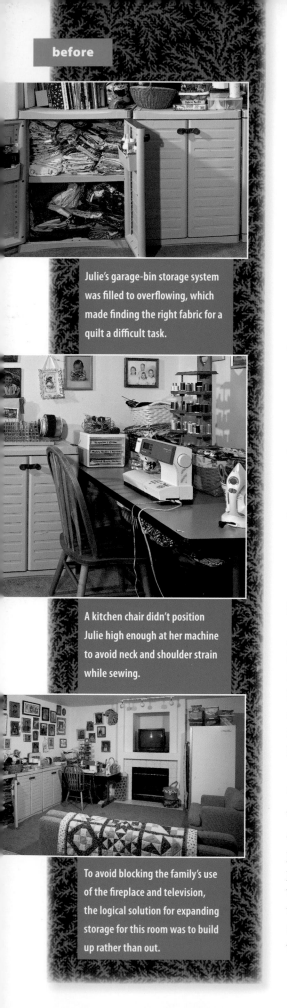

Julie's garage-bin storage system was filled to overflowing, which made finding the right fabric for a quilt a difficult task.

A kitchen chair didn't position Julie high enough at her machine to avoid neck and shoulder strain while sewing.

To avoid blocking the family's use of the fireplace and television, the logical solution for expanding storage for this room was to build up rather than out.

- One of Julie's biggest problems was that she didn't know what she had and where it was stored. Notions were in the living room, overflow fabric was in boxes in the garage, some supplies were stored under her bed, and patterns were in a file cabinet in the dining room. Julie's scraps were stuffed in plastic trash bags that she stored under her sewing table. Getting started on a new project wasted lots of time and created a mess as she tried to find what she needed.

- Julie's kitchen island was the perfect height for rotary cutting and it was fairly near her sewing space. However, Julie would frequently start a quilt project by cleaning the kitchen and then refuse to cook until her project was complete. This was not so much of a problem for her, but her family might have preferred another solution!

- Along with a dedicated cutting space, Julie wanted a cutting system to be a high priority in her makeover budget. She was having a difficult time remaining accurate during rotary cutting and was intimidated by the idea of cutting triangles. Julie felt that a cutting system would help solve that problem.

- Julie used an ordinary kitchen chair that wasn't adjustable for sewing. Because she is tall, Julie enjoyed the large amount of legroom that her office table afforded, but she sat too low.

- Julie likes to save scraps. She has even received bags of scraps from friends and neighbors, so it was important that she have something better than a garbage bag for storage.

the solutions

Julie's original concept for her quilt studio was to take over the entire family room and set her sewing table in the center of the room. She was frustrated with storage issues and felt that her only solution was to kick her family out entirely. She knew she needed more storage but did not see the potential for "going vertical" rather than eating up floor space. Together we decided that her location was excellent, but she needed a large storage wall.

replace too-deep storage with easy-access cupboards

We replaced the deep, plastic storage cabinets with 14"-deep modular cabinets that came ready to assemble. Julie's husband, Ross, selected pine cabinets over other options, because he knew he could easily find pine boards to build matching shelves and countertops. Julie felt it would be hard to stay neat and tidy, so she preferred solid doors for the majority of the cabinets. To break up the imposing look of a wall of solid wood cabinets, we outfitted two of the cabinets with glass doors, which create a colorful backdrop for her studio.

Located in the same spot as the previous storage bins, the new pine cabinets more than double the storage capacity while taking up very little additional floor space. Only the new cutting peninsula juts out farther into the family room.

increase storage capacity by installing wall-mounted cabinets

With this design, I tripled the number of cabinets Julie could use for fabric and supplies without using more floor space.

combine cutting and storage with a designated peninsula

Two of the cabinets are placed on risers and set back to back, forming a much needed cutting peninsula. Ross built the cutting-table surface and the bookshelves above it.

create a space for bulk storage

To handle bulk storage (sewing machine cover, batting rolls, and other large items), one of the cutting table cabinets is on glides and can slide out to expose a deep storage pocket behind the cutting cabinets next to the wall.

install a double-duty workstation

Julie's new cutting peninsula doubles as a pressing surface when she has

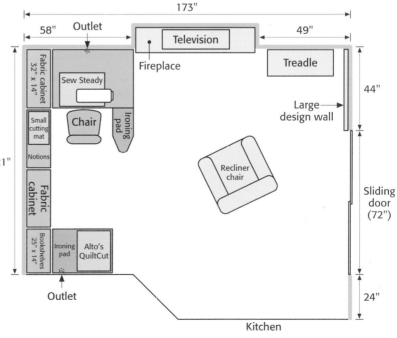

Julie's new quilt studio layout

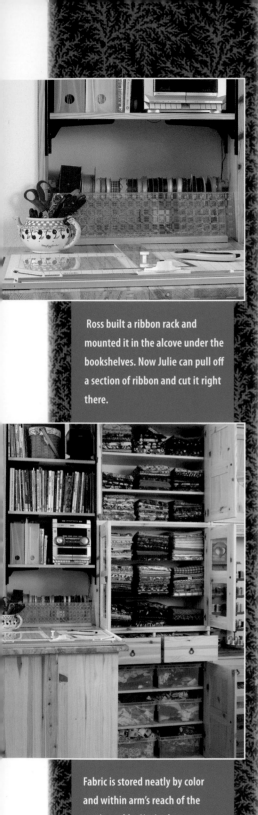

Ross built a ribbon rack and mounted it in the alcove under the bookshelves. Now Julie can pull off a section of ribbon and cut it right there.

Fabric is stored neatly by color and within arm's reach of the cutting table. Notice how scraps are sorted in see-through tubs by color, too, for easy access for Julie's next scrap quilt.

large amounts of fabric to press. She simply replaces the cutting mat with a pressing pad on the surface.

incorporate the quilter's work triangle

The new quilt studio incorporates a U-shaped workstation for sewing with a clamp-on ironing board to the right and a secondary cutting surface to the left of the machine. Julie purchased an adjustable office chair, which was a simple solution to her ergonomic issues. The chair rolls easily on her wood-laminate flooring and allows her to move freely between cutting, pressing, and sewing. She has easy access to a block design wall and to a thread rack above her secondary cutting space. She also has plenty of drawers for storing sewing notions, which she can easily reach while seated.

plan for good ergonomics

Julie found that using an angled footrest helped contain her sewing pedal and reduce stress on her right leg. Since her sewing machine sat on top of her office table, she also purchased a clear acrylic table to extend her machine bed. This helps her support the fabric when machine quilting.

customize a scrap-storage solution

For the all-important scrap storage, Julie bought a dozen clear plastic bins and lined them up in a row on the floor. She then sorted her scraps by color and dropped them into the appropriate bin. The scrap bins are stored behind doors yet are within reach of the cutting table, so she can drop scraps into the appropriate bin as she creates them. When Julie needs a scrap of a certain color, it is much easier to search through a clear plastic bin of one fabric color than to dig through an entire garbage bag.

additional benefits

Julie's new quilt studio solved her major problems by adding a lot of extra storage space without taking up additional floor space. This allowed room for a family member or two to join her in the family room/quilt studio.

- Because she didn't have to take up the entire space with storage furniture, Julie had room to relocate her antique treadle sewing machine from a hallway to a prominent location in her quilt studio.

- Julie had space on a blank wall in her family room for a larger design wall. Her television, stereo, and comfortable armchair for hand sewing and knitting give Julie the oasis of tranquility she needed.

Fat quarters have their own storage system, tucked neatly in drawers next to the scrap bins. Above the drawers is a secondary cutting spot near the sewing machine, and a design wall for placing blocks that have been trimmed to size.

the bottom line

Ready-to-assemble furniture can be a great way to save money. Julie's large storage wall holds a volume of nearly 66 cubic feet.

Total cost: about $1,000

Where the money went: nine modular storage units, building materials for shelves, sewing chair, Sew Steady table, portable design wall, easy chair for hand sewing, Alto cutting system

Lessons learned: When considering your own quilt studio design, do not forget to look up. As our storage systems overflow, we tend to make stacks on the floor and other horizontal surfaces, making our rooms feel smaller due to the loss of floor space. Get everything off the floor and onto shelving. Make sure the shelf depth fits the items you need to store. Put your most frequently used items within easiest reach. Remember to choose closed storage for items that are hard to keep tidy. Most importantly, know your priorities so you are sure to get the results you need.

Julie retired the family room furniture in favor of a comfy armchair, which is a perfect spot for hand sewing, knitting, or simply watching television. Notice the new larger design wall in the background too.

custom-built solutions

MY SEWING TABLE IS WONDERFUL. Not only is it the perfect height, but everything I need is right there within reach. I am pretty stress free when I sew now. But I have a new problem: I never want to leave my studio!
—*Laurie Giddings*

the situation

Laurie has a cute little country home that exudes warmth and vintage charm. Her space is extremely precious and her quilting studio serves a dual purpose—it is also a guest bedroom. To make the most of a small space, a homebuilt Murphy bed folds down on one wall, and built-in shelves on the window wall house her fabric and book collections.

- Although Laurie was trying to stay organized, her supplies were beginning to overflow her tool- and pattern-storage systems. As a result, the small room felt even smaller due to the extreme amount of visual clutter.

- Laurie experiences shoulder and neck pain due to an unrelated physical condition, and the situation is often

before

The variety of styles and sizes of storage containers visually overwhelmed the sewing area.

The 8' x 8' design wall was one feature of the original room setup that Laurie intended to keep.

The foldaway Murphy bed was located just inside the doorway. Storage shelves took advantage of the space above the bed but blocked the view into the room from the doorway.

aggravated by her quilting. Laurie is a few inches taller than average, and her store-bought cutting table was too low for her, causing her to hunch over while cutting. Conversely, the banquet table she used for machine sewing was too high, causing her to tense her shoulders during machine sewing and quilting.

• Laurie likes to watch movies while working at her sewing machine, but her large television was located at such an angle that she had to turn her head and look up to see the screen, increasing neck strain.

the solutions

Laurie's husband, John, is a talented woodworker. After we identified that Laurie needed cabinetry built to house all of her supplies so that we could reduce visual clutter and improve the ergonomics of her work space, Laurie drafted the plans, and John was ready to build to her specifications.

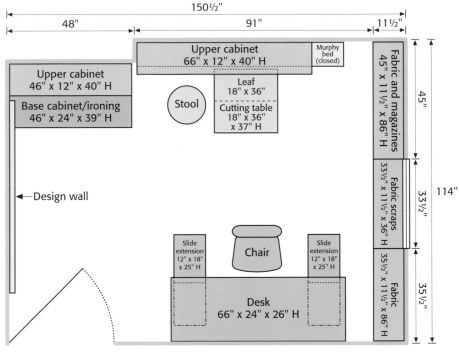

Laurie's new quilt studio layout

make use of wall space in tight quarters

We increased storage by using the vertical space. Cutting tables and pressing surfaces had to be portable so they could be stowed away beneath her cabinets and incorporate storage underneath.

With the sewing table and Murphy bed swapping locations, the room now has lots more room for built-in storage. A roll-away cutting table (right) moves out of the way when the bed is needed. The pressing table (left) stows away between the top cupboard and base cabinet when not in use.

create one focal point to reduce visual clutter

Laurie's existing storage wall was filled with fabric that could have acted as a focal point for her room, but the visual clutter of the other items drew attention away from the beautiful fabric. The layout we chose for Laurie's room kept her fabric in the same spot, but because we put almost everything else behind closed doors, the fabric now added visual punch.

gain visual space by decluttering the entryway

Another trick to making any room seem bigger is to make the entry feel as open as possible. Originally, the Murphy bed and open shelving were located on the wall right by the door, blocking the view of the fabric. When we moved the majority of storage to the wall opposite the door, the wall of fabric became a focal point. In its new location, the Murphy bed made use of recessed wall space in the area underneath the storage cabinet. The new cutting table could be rolled away to convert the room into a guest bedroom.

Laurie designed her sewing table with a drop leaf in back that can be raised for machine quilting. The pullout surfaces on either side of the sewing chair create a handy U-shaped work area.

The sewing table does double-duty as a light box. Laurie placed a Plexiglas insert on the machine cutout and an inexpensive light rope underneath for easy pattern tracing.

replace inappropriate furniture for better ergonomics

Replacing Laurie's 6'-long banquet table with an appropriately sized sewing table freed up floor space and reduced visual clutter. The custom-built table has some wonderful features to meet her needs, but what is most important is that it is built to the correct height for Laurie, allowing her to work pain free for longer periods of time. When she is in a seated position, her TV is just slightly below eye level, similar to the height of her sewing machine. Everything she needs is within reach. The smaller drawers hold thread, sewing machine feet, and other notions for machine sewing, while the large drawer holds her serger and related supplies.

use pullout surfaces to take advantage of the small space

When the sewing table is closed, everything is quite compact, but when they're needed, Laurie can use the sewing table's two pullouts—similar to kitchen breadboards—to make a U-shaped workstation. In addition, the sewing table is on rolling casters and has a hinged extension on the back, allowing Laurie to support a large quilt when machine quilting or attaching binding, again helping to reduce neck and shoulder stress.

think storage, storage, storage

Since Laurie's room doesn't have a closet, every bit of space needed to be used. The new cutting table houses all the large, flat items found in her studio. This concept is copied from the cookie-sheet cabinet designs found in many kitchens. The cutting table doubles as a design space, and when her drafting board is not in use, it stows in the cabinet below. She keeps her pencils, templates, and other drafting supplies in the handy drawers that are accessible from both sides of her cabinet.

hide-away surfaces add value and save space

Laurie's pressing station is another unique feature of her room that solves all sorts of problems. This cabinet is built on furniture glides so it can be pulled out from the wall when needed for pressing or slipped back in place where it blends with the wall of cabinets. It has a flip-up shelf to hold an iron and drawers to hold supplies.

The cabinet below Laurie's pressing station is for bulk storage—machine cases, batting, and other large items. A wooden rack (similar to a wine rack) is suspended from one corner to house Laurie's rolled interfacing and stabilizers. The bins above the pressing station hide her iron, spray bottle, and cans of sizing and adhesives; the baskets hold her patterns. The glass door panels of her upper shelves allow you to peek at her colorful quilt tops and backing fabrics.

In this makeover, no opportunity to increase storage went to waste. Even the small cutting cart with its drop-leaf extension provides concealed storage for larger items such as Laurie's drafting table, portable ironing board, and Alto cutting system.

The cupboards above the cutting table and Murphy bed are the perfect depth for storing books and magazines. Removing them from the fabric shelves gives Laurie more room for her fabric stash.

additional benefits

All the extra storage that we designed and built gave Laurie the room to organize her visually cluttered fabric wall in a new way.

- She was able to move her books closer to her design space, freeing up shelf space for her scraps, which are sorted by color.

- White fiberboard boxes now store works in progress on the highest shelves above her fabric. Laurie labeled all the boxes so she can quickly find what she needs.

- Laurie also organized her magazines into labeled holders and located them on her lowest shelves, because she doesn't consult them frequently. The shelf below the window holds a large ruler basket to corral the majority of her cutting tools and rulers. The largest and most frequently used rulers are hung on the side of her cutting table within easy reach.

- John made a clever gadget that lets Laurie turn her sewing table into a light table. A light rope slips into the machine opening under a solid Plexiglas insert for easy pattern tracing.

- With all the new cabinetry, Laurie was still able to maintain a guest room with country charm. Painted bead-board cupboards, punched-tin quilt block accents, and awning-striped fabric details are just a few of the ways she made this quilt studio uniquely hers.

With the cutting table rolled out of the way, there's plenty of room for the Murphy bed to be opened up and put to good use.

the bottom line

Custom-built furniture and storage is a fabulous way to get exactly what you need for your quilt studio. If you do not have the skills and equipment needed, you could hire a cabinetmaker to build custom items.

Total cost: under $2,000

Where the money went: lumber, hardware, paint, storage bins, decorative fabric

Lessons learned: Even if you cannot afford custom cabinetry, you can employ some of the same techniques used here to reduce visual clutter. Put items behind closed doors. Balance your stored items symmetrically. Use single-colored opaque storage and magazine boxes. These simple changes will improve the feel of your quilting studio.

Laurie's height is above average, but her ideal sewing table height is just 26" high. Keep in mind that your ideal sewing height has just as much to do with the length of your arms as it does with your overall height. Your palms need to rest on the table surface when your elbows are bent at 90°. If the table is too high, you'll end up scrunching your shoulders when you sew.

Below the stowed pressing table is a cabinet for bulk storage. Above is a cupboard where Laurie stores finished quilt tops and larger pieces of fabric.

ready-to-assemble solutions for a fabric collector

LOIS FULFILLED ALL OF MY NEEDS for my room. Now my family, cats, and I enjoy it tremendously. It has become my sanctuary.—*Terry Martin*

the situation

Terry is a prolific quiltmaker and quilting-book author. She works full time by day, and between that and being a wife and mother, writes books evenings and weekends. She is also an avid fabric collector. Terry's quilting studio is a 16' x 21' bonus room located on the second floor of her house. The large space was devoted entirely to her craft. She already had a design wall, a guest sewing table, and tons of storage.

- Terry's major problem was fabric storage. Shelving units were stuffed to the gills, and fabric was overflowing onto the floor. Terry felt very strongly that having her fabric visible was an important inspiration for her. She liked to keep fabric collections together and wanted a storage method that was flexible enough to allow for future purchases or for grouping fabrics selected for a particular quilt.

Shallow shelves of different heights and finishes made the fabric storage system look jumbled.

Placed back to back, the two sewing tables didn't provide the convenience of an L-shaped setup.

Two large storage racks served in place of a closet, but the appearance of items in assorted sizes added to the visual clutter in the room.

- Terry also wanted a place in her studio where she could hand sew. She already had a television and videocassette player so she could watch movies while she was machine sewing. But she was determined that her studio would also include a love seat for doing handwork. Her studio was already full to the bursting point, so it seemed from the start that a love seat wouldn't fit without removing some other pieces of furniture.

the solutions

We divided the room into four quadrants and treated her large room as four smaller zones: a fabric zone with a cutting table and fabric storage, a machine-sewing zone with guest sewing space and design wall access, a sitting room with lighting for hand sewing, and an office zone for book creation. Each zone needed to be self sufficient for the activity that would occur there. Terry was so excited to get into her new studio that she rearranged her existing furniture into the planned layout right away. She discovered that she loved the feel of the new configuration and was ready to purchase the new furniture needed to increase her storage capability.

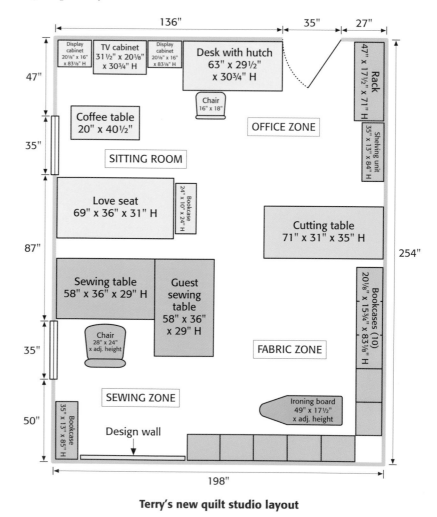

Terry's new quilt studio layout

after

reduce visual clutter with matching storage units

Terry's old fabric-storage bookcases varied in depth, width, and height. Only one was suitable for storing fabric; the rest were too shallow. She decided to retire the existing shelving in favor of narrow bookcases that would fit two stacks of folded fabric side by side. Each new bookcase was 15" deep, had adjustable shelves, and was 83" tall to make use of as much vertical space as possible.

fold fabric uniformly for maximum impact

New shelves were a first step in reducing the visual clutter. But to really showcase Terry's fabric collection, all the fabric needed to be folded uniformly. Surprisingly, it took Terry and her friends over 200 hours to fold it all, but the result is so stunning that Terry is committed to keeping it organized.

store fabric bolts separately

Terry's new shelves are great for folded fabric, but less efficient for fabric bolts. We kept one of her shallow bookcases for that purpose.

use wire storage racks in lieu of a closet

Since Terry's quilt studio doesn't have a closet, we also kept one of her deep wire-shelved racks for storing plastic bins of fat quarters and bulky items. But, to free up more floor space, we removed the shelves from one unit and placed them on the other unit; this gave her the

Fabric is arranged on one wall by color and on the adjacent wall in categories such as florals, batiks, and so on. This makes it easy to see at a glance which colors are running low or where to look for a particular fabric when inspiration hits.

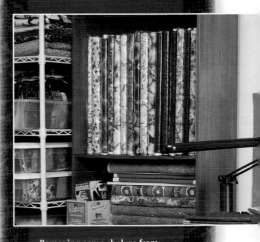

Removing some shelves from a bookcase makes it a suitable storage unit for fabric bolts.

Fat quarters store neatly in shallow plastic tubs placed on the wire storage rack.

same number of shelves, but she had one less unit. With the shelves spaced more closely together, we had sufficient room to place Terry's plastic bins of fat quarters on the most accessible shelves. The bins work almost like drawers—easy to pull out to peruse fabric. Terry uses the top shelf for folded quilts and the bottom shelf for scrap bins.

position furniture to create a work triangle

Terry's cutting table was a good height for her. We merely repositioned it near the fabric wall so that she could easily pull fabric for cutting. We added a wall-mounted ruler rack beside her cutting space and tucked plastic storage bins under her table along with machine covers and other bulk items. Terry's design wall is behind her sewing table, where she can swivel and roll toward it from her work triangle.

enhance lighting with task lights

The room lighting was excellent, but Terry wanted additional lighting at her cutting space. She chose a dual-duty lamp that came with two bases: a clamp-on base to attach to the cutting table and a floor base to use by the handwork seating.

adjust the seat for easy ergonomics

A wooden banquet table gave Terry plenty of legroom, but it was a bit high for comfortable sewing. An easy, no-cost fix was to simply raise the seat of her adjustable office chair.

put everything within reach with a U-shaped set up

The new room layout made a U-shaped workstation at her sewing machine. Her guest table doubles as a secondary cutting surface that's accessible while seated at her machine. We located rolling file cabinets under both her sewing table and the guest table. These cabinets store tools within easy reach of the machine and serve as secondary cutting and pressing surfaces. Now Terry has a complete secondary work triangle at her machine.

make use of out-of-the-way spaces with rolling-cart storage

The guest sewing space doubles as Terry's quilt design space. In the rolling file cabinet under the table, she keeps graph paper, a calculator, and colored pencils, as well as file folders of design ideas. Her design space is close to her fabric so she can audition her ideas in living color.

divide a large space into smaller work zones

As Terry's books approach completion, she can move to her computer workstation. She has space at her computer station for her notebooks and art supplies, and plenty of lateral-file storage under her TV stand for more files. Her printer/scanner unit is located on the upper shelf of the hutch, keeping precious desktop space free.

The new seating area is perfect for watching TV or hand stitching. The adjacent office zone completes this side of the room.

This bird's-eye view shows the U-shaped sewing area with secondary cutting and pressing stations.

A small bookcase next to the love seat holds quilting magazines—and provides a spot to set a beverage—making this a perfect spot for browsing for new ideas.

additional benefits

Terry liked to watch old movies while sewing, but she was generally working in her quilt studio by herself. She was used to the solitude but didn't realize that she was missing out on time with her family. On Terry's first day of sewing in her new studio, her teenage daughter, McKenzie, settled in the love seat to watch movies with her. They chatted and laughed throughout the movie while Terry sewed. This was a wonderful benefit that she hadn't anticipated.

the bottom line

Terry had a large room and plenty of fabric and supplies to house. She kept on budget by selecting ready-to-assemble furniture.

Total cost: less than $2,000

Where the money went: ten bookcases for fabric, a love seat, a computer workstation, a television stand, two curio cabinets, two rolling file cabinets

Lessons learned: To gain maximum storage for the least cost, focus your makeover solutions on ready-to-assemble furniture. Avoiding changes to flooring, lighting, and sewing tables keeps makeover costs lower.

Room layout in a large space can create a look that's deceiving. By working from Terry's graph paper floor plan, we learned that there was more space for furniture than we originally thought would be possible.

If you have a large room, divide it into smaller, more manageable work triangles for the most efficient use of your space.

Terry's existing cutting table didn't offer lots of storage, but placed along the wall, it provides a good spot below for storing her notions bins.

converting a garage into a dream studio

MY FAVORITE PART OF THE WHOLE PROJECT is the fact that we made the commitment to create a space in which to play. Now, for the first time, we have a bright, pretty, inviting space that we can enjoy together.
—*Mary Green*

THIS NEW QUILTING STUDIO IS SO LAVISH in light, space, and energy that we both have the freedom to work at our own pace and in our own style.
—*Stan Green*

the situation

Stan and Mary Green are an unusual couple in that they are both quilters. Now, you might think it would be wonderful to share this hobby with your spouse, because you could talk about your common passion for fabric collecting and quilt design. But imagine a small quilting studio with the two of you working on projects at the same time. If you've ever tried to cook dinner in a tiny kitchen with your spouse, you know that sharing a work

before

space can be a recipe for disaster. Stan and Mary chose to take turns using their previous quilting studio, because it was just too crowded for two people to work at the same time.

After sharing space for so long, they knew that they had very different work styles. Mary enjoyed being neat and tidy, with all items put away when not in use. Stan liked to create in a more cluttered space. Mary usually finished one project before starting the next, while Stan had multiple projects going at once. Sharing a cutting table meant that Mary would have to clean up Stan's various works in progress before she could get to her own project.

- The Greens used an extra bedroom for a joint quilt studio, and due to the small space, they shared absolutely everything: one sewing machine, one cutting table, one ironing board, one design wall, and one closet stacked with fabric.

- Because Mary is left-handed and Stan is right-handed, whenever they swapped turns in the studio they had to move tools and supplies to the correct side of the cutting and sewing tables—and even the ironing board—so that they could each work efficiently.

- Interestingly enough, they have very different tastes in fabric. In that one closet were two separate piles of fabric—his and hers. Stan and Mary tried to be respectful of one another's fabric and not dip into the other person's collection without permission. But the stash on the wide closet shelves had become somewhat jumbled, so it was hard for me to tell whose fabric was whose.

- Both Stan and Mary are book collectors. Throughout the house they had multiple bookcases of quilting and knitting books, not to mention gardening books, cookbooks, and novels.

- Just as they did with the sewing space, the Greens shared a design wall and had to remove one another's projects before using the wall for their own designs. When planning their new quilt studio, they were adamant about not sharing anything—except the space itself. In addition to needing separate sewing tables so that they could sew at the same time, they wanted separate design walls, fabric-storage space, and cutting tables.

the solutions

Stan and Mary own a weekend home that will become their permanent residence once they're retired. When they bought the house, it had an interesting but unnecessary feature: an extra two-car garage. They used one of the two-car garages for parking; the other was slated to become a quilt studio. But because the space was a garage, it had its own set of challenges: not enough outlets, not enough lighting, an unfinished concrete floor, and so on.

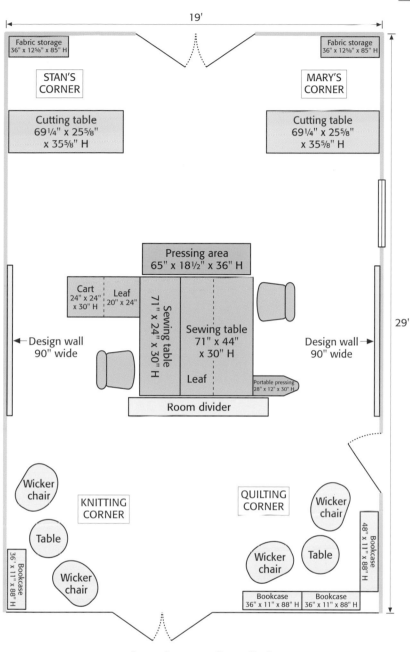

19'

Fabric storage
36" x 12⅝" x 85" H

Fabric storage
36" x 12⅝" x 85" H

STAN'S CORNER

MARY'S CORNER

Cutting table
69¼" x 25⅝"
x 35⅝" H

Cutting table
69¼" x 25⅝"
x 35⅝" H

29'

Pressing area
65" x 18½" x 36" H

Cart
24" x 24"
x 30" H

Leaf
20" x 24"

Sewing table
71" x 24" x 30" H

Sewing table
71" x 44"
x 30" H

Leaf

Portable pressing
28" x 12" x 30" H

← Design wall
90" wide

Design wall →
90" wide

Room divider

Wicker chair

KNITTING CORNER

QUILTING CORNER

Wicker chair

Table

Wicker chair

Table

Bookcase
48" x 11" x 88" H

Wicker chair

Bookcase
36" x 11" x 88" H

Wicker chair

Bookcase
36" x 11" x 88" H

Bookcase
36" x 11" x 88" H

Stan and Mary's new quilt studio layout

A purchased buffet is topped with an ironing surface. The buffet provides plenty of storage below as well as enough surface area for pressing a wide quilt top.

divide and conquer a large space with work zones

The Greens' new quilt studio is very balanced. They chose the same furniture for both quilters and placed it symmetrically in the room. We divided the room into quadrants with a center island for sewing and pressing.

position design walls within easy reach

We positioned a design wall directly behind each sewing space, so Stan and Mary can turn and roll their sewing chairs when picking blocks off their own design walls.

Plastic basket liners with dividers help Mary keep her scrap basket organized by strip width.

create easy access for two in shared spaces

The Greens share a large pressing surface, but they can plug in multiple irons at the same time and use opposite ends of the pressing station.

maximize natural light with skylights

Stan installed two large skylights over the sewing space to ensure plenty of natural light during the daytime. Two main light fixtures with compact fluorescent lights provide nighttime lighting for sewing. Track lighting is focused on each design wall and cutting table—the places where more light is needed. To make this large room part of the overall living space and take away the feel of a garage, large French doors now open into the living room on one end of the room and into the garden on the other. These doors also let in natural daylight.

plan ahead for electrical needs

Because the sewing tables are placed back to back in the center of the room, it wasn't sufficient to simply add wall outlets for the sewing machines and irons. We needed access to electricity in the interior of the room so that no one would trip over extension cords running from wall outlets to the sewing and pressing stations. The solution was for Stan to design and build a columned room divider to bring power to the center of the room. We devoted one complete electrical circuit to the pressing station so that electronic sewing machines and portable lighting won't flicker with the power surges caused by the iron.

call a rolling cart into service

Stan's sewing space has a rolling storage cart that can be called into duty as a secondary cutting or pressing surface, or as a design desk. It works great for supporting a large quilt during machine quilting too. Stan designs his own patterns, so the drawers in this unit hold his sketch pads, pencils, drawing templates, and rulers.

choose storage containers to suit your needs and style

Stan uses sea grass baskets under his cutting table to contain his works in progress. With many projects going at the same time, he has eight baskets, each containing a different project. We selected a different type of basket for Mary's cutting space, because she prefers to use them to store fabric scraps. She likes to cut leftovers from a current project into common strip widths and square sizes for future projects. One basket contains strips in three different widths, one contains squares in three different sizes, and the last one has larger chunks of scrap fabric divided into lights, mediums, and darks.

organize storage for easy retrieval

Mary also uses handy drawer dividers with handles so they can be removed and carried like toolboxes wherever she needs them. One tray contains hand quilting and marking tools, another corrals basting and binding supplies, and the last holds everything needed for hand sewing and appliqué.

A portable, clamp-on ironing board gives Mary plenty of space to cut and press blocks while seated. Her design wall is within easy reach, located just behind her sewing station.

Dividers are a good way to keep a larger space organized.

convert a long worktable into a space that's L- or U-shaped

Mary's sewing station has a portable table that she can attach to her main sewing table for a secondary pressing or cutting station. This table has an adjustable-height leg and can be taken along to quilt classes and retreats for an instant L-shaped workstation.

additional benefits

With such a large space, the Greens can now use their new studio for several additional purposes, including reading, knitting, and rug hooking.

- Now they store all their craft books in one place. Because the Greens have such an extensive collection, they sorted their books by craft, with quilting books in one corner of the room and knitting books in another, all alphabetized for easy retrieval. A small table can hold thread and scissors to make the space productive for hand quilting. An adjustable quilting frame is ready for Stan or Mary whenever one of them gets an urge to hand quilt.

The quilting nook has room for hand stitching and browsing through books for new ideas. The shelves allow space for a growing library.

- Mary's knitting corner has room for her knitting books and yarn. The closed-door cabinets contain skeins of yarn just waiting for a project, while baskets of yarn nearby make it easy to retrieve another ball when needed. A small table gives Mary a place to set her teacup, and a floor lamp ensures that she has adequate lighting. She stores knitting magazines in a basket near her chair.

- The Greens' quilt studio has a lot of versatility built into the design. All furnishings are on castors or glides, and the room can be reconfigured for hosting a gathering. The sewing tables can be turned and rolled to the outside walls. The pressing table can be pushed against the room divider so that all quilters have easy access. Multiple banquet tables can be set up to accommodate up to 10 quilters for a retreat.

- There is also room for growth in the Greens' quilt studio. The cupboards can accommodate future fabric purchases, and if the cupboards continue to fill up, there is room for an additional cabinet on each side of the French doors. The bookcases are only partially filled, and most of the cabinets beneath them are currently empty, so Stan and Mary can acquire new books (or fabric or yarn) without wondering where it will be stored.

The knitting nook houses knitting books and magazines on shelves, with yarn tucked away in the closed cupboards.

the bottom line

After eight months of hard work and determination, Stan and Mary moved their quilting from a 100-square-foot spare bedroom into their 550-square-foot dream studio.

Total cost: approximately $10,000

Where the money went: furniture—two cutting tables, two fabric storage units, one pressing buffet, one new sewing table, sewing and occasional chairs (approximately $5,000); construction materials—subflooring, floor tiles, track lighting, electrical outlets, skylights, two sets of French doors, drywall, insulation, outdoor siding to frame in the new walls where the garage doors were removed (approximately $5,000).

Lessons learned: A garage conversion is a large project that entails a significant commitment of time and money. Doing the work yourself saves a lot of money, but it costs you a lot of time. The Greens calculate that hiring contractors would have easily cost three times what they spent.

If you intend to embark on a project of this size, do a lot of planning up front. Sequence your work in logical stages so that you don't have to spend time backtracking. For example, don't paint the walls until your lighting and electrical work are complete. Schedule work parties for large jobs, and invite friends to help out. Remember that any project can become a chore if it's the only activity in your life for a long period of time; pace yourself so that you'll have time for fun along the way.

This columned bookcase houses the electrical supply for the sewing and pressing stations, and visually separates the quilt studio from the living room.

products used in makeovers

CATEGORY	PRODUCT	SOURCE	PAGE
Computer Furniture	Anton desk with hutch	Ikea	79
Cutting Furniture and Accessories	Alto Pro cutting mat	Alto's	7, 86, 87
	Alto QuiltCut2	Alto's	60, 63, 64
	Buffet	The Bramble Company	25, 36, 52
	Hanging ruler holder	Nancy's Notions	30, 78, 81
	Moda ruler basket	Hancock's of Paducah	30, 66
	Monster cutting mat	Sewer's Dream Outlet	6, 30, 69
	Omnigrid FoldAway portable cutting and pressing station	Nancy's Notions	42, 46, 47
	Omnigrid ruler rack	Nancy's Notions	48
	Varde kitchen base cabinet	Ikea	25, 86, 87
Design Wall	Felted quilt wall	Keepsake Quilting Inc.	42, 45, 46
	Quilter's BlockButler design wall	BlockButler Inc.	65
Fabric Storage and Accessories	Husar pine cabinet	Ikea	23, 60, 63
	Martha linen cupboard	The Bramble Company	36, 49, 52
	Tunhem cabinet	Ikea	26, 34, 54, 58, 59, 77
	Visdalen cabinet	Ikea	25, 82
Lighting	TrueColor Arial 2-in-1 lamp	Ott-Lite Technology	77, 81
	TrueColor task lamp	Ott-Lite Technology	63
	Ultralux floor lamp	Full Spectrum Solutions Inc.	59
Pressing Furniture and Accessories	Ironing board cover	MeasureMatic Inc.	69, 72
	Markor sideboard	Ikea	26, 85
	Portable pressing table	Huntercraft	23, 25, 61
	Pressing cabinet	Improvements	27

CATEGORY	PRODUCT	SOURCE	PAGE
Sewing Furniture and Accessories	Custom oak sewing table	Northwest Sewing	88
	Deluxe sewing center	Horn of America	9
	Effektiv drawer unit	Ikea	74, 79, 80
	Galant table	Ikea	13, 55, 57
	Koala sewing station chair	Koala Cabinets	9
	Neez-Ez	Nancy's Notions	65
	Sew Steady cabinet insert	Dream World Inc.	67, 70
	Sew Steady portable table	Dream World Inc.	23, 25, 61
Small Storage Solutions	Bread basket	The Longaberger Company	23, 45, 61
	Cake basket	The Longaberger Company	66
	Cutlery tray	Ikea	10, 87
	Darning basket	The Longaberger Company	45
	Fabric-covered boxes	Clearview Designs	11, 30
	Kassett boxes with lids	Ikea	41, 51, 66
	Knuff magazine files	Ikea	41, 66
	Market basket	The Longaberger Company	9
	Medium berry basket	The Longaberger Company	45
	Medium gathering basket	The Longaberger Company	51
	Pen Pal basket	The Longaberger Company	88
	Project boxes	Great Little Box Company	30, 51
	Scrap bins	Storables USA Inc.	64
	Seagrass basket	Pier 1 Imports	86, 87
	Serve-it-up tray	The Longaberger Company	86
	Small gathering basket	The Longaberger Company	23, 61, 45, 90
	Spring basket	The Longaberger Company	63
	Storage solutions	The Longaberger Company	30, 86, 87
	TV Time basket	The Longaberger Company	87

product sources

Alto's
800-225-2497
www.quiltcut.com
Alto QuiltCut Pro and QuiltCut2 cutting systems and tools for precision rotary cutting

BlockButler Inc.
425-644-4242
www.blockbutler.com
Self-stick, washable design walls

The Bramble Company
608-897-2186
www.brambleco.com
Buffets, tables, and storage cabinets

Clearview Designs
360-668-5609
www.clearview-designs.com
Quilt studio designs and tools to organize workspaces

Dream World Inc.
800-837-3261
www.dreamworld-inc.com
Plexiglas cabinet inserts and extension tables for all brands of sewing machines

Full Spectrum Solutions Inc.
888-574-7014
www.fullspectrumsolutions.com
Lighting fixtures and bulbs

Great Little Box Company
800-661-3377
www.greatlittlebox.com
Corrugated boxes

Hancock's of Paducah
800-845-8723
www.hancocks-paducah.com
Ruler baskets, notions, and fabric

Horn of America
800-882-8845
www.hornofamerica.com
Sewing machine cabinets, cutting tables, and storage furniture

Huntercraft
206-781-4836
www.huntercraft.com
Portable ironing boards, sewing accessories, quilt designs, and custom woodworking

Ikea
800-434-4532
www.ikea.com
Furniture and home-organization products

Improvements
800-642-2112
www.ImprovementsCatalog.com
Ironing board cabinets and other home-organization products

Keepsake Quilting Inc.
800-865-9458
www.keepsakequilting.com
Quilt design walls, notions, and fabric

Koala Cabinets
877-554-4739
www.koalacabinets.com
Sewing cabinets, cutting tables, storage furniture, and sewing chairs

The Longaberger Company
740-321-3447
www.longaberger.com
Baskets for organizing

MeasureMatic Inc.
707-745-1138
www.miracleironing.com
Ironing board covers to fit standard and custom sizes